The FERMENTED Food Cookbook FOR BEGINNERS

The Fermented Food Cookbook for Beginners: Rebalance Your Gut, Fortify Immunity & Boost Energy | Foolproof, Doctor-Approved Recipes with Step-by-Step Techniques for Safe, Delicious Results

COPYRIGHT © 2026

TABLE OF CONTENTS

CHAPTER 3

CHAPTER 4

CHAPTER 5

CHAPTER 6

CHAPTER 7

CHAPTER 8

CHAPTER 9

CHAPTER 10

Your Exclusive Bonuses Are Waiting!

Thank you for choosing this cookbook — you've just taken a big step toward mastering the art of fermentation and filling your pantry with safe, delicious, and nutrient-packed ferments.

But there's even more for you! As a reader, you also get exclusive free bonuses designed to make your fermenting journey easier, safer, and far more rewarding.

Inside your bonus pack you'll find:

- ✅ Say goodbye to dead cultures with the Starter Care & Rescue Kit
- ✅ Stay in control with Photocopiable Batch Sheets (Small-Batch / Family)
- ✅ Unlock chef-level flavor with the Flavor Pairing & Brine Spice Atlas

…and much more.

How to get them?
Simply go to the last page of this book, where you'll find clear instructions. With just a quick scan, you'll instantly unlock your full bonus pack.

Don't miss these resources — they're the perfect companion to this book and will give you the confidence, inspiration, and tools to ferment like a pro every single day.

INTRODUCTION

1. HOW TO USE THIS BOOK IN 5 MINUTES

This book was designed for anyone who wants quick, reliable results without wading through endless theory. In just a few pages, you'll find the essential foundations for fermenting safely and successfully—even if you're a complete beginner.

Here are the three key steps to get you started:

Choosing Between "Small-Batch" and "Family" Recipes

- Small-Batch recipes are perfect if you're experimenting for the first time or want to work with smaller quantities, minimizing waste.
- Family recipes are meant for larger batches, ideal for sharing at the table or storing for several weeks.

Calculating Salt Percentage and Using a Scale

Salt is the backbone of every fermentation: too little and you risk contamination, too much and you'll suppress the beneficial microbes. This book will walk you step by step through calculating the right amount—generally between 2% and 3% of the total ingredient weight. To get it right every time, skip the spoons: a simple digital scale is the tool that guarantees consistent results.

Temperatures, Timelines, and Tasting Notes

The ideal temperature for most home ferments is between 64 °F and 72 °F (18 22 °C). Timelines vary by recipe and season: you might enjoy kimchi in just a few days, while miso requires months of patient waiting.

Never rely solely on the calendar: taste, look, and smell. Your palate and nose are the best guides to decide when a ferment has reached the flavor you love.

Start here, with these simple rules. In less than five minutes, you'll be ready to dive into the recipes that follow with confidence and curiosity.

2. FERMENTATION ESSENTIALS FOR BEGINNERS

Friendly Microbes (LAB), in Plain Language

At the heart of fermentation are lactic acid bacteria (LAB). Don't be put off by the name—they're your invisible allies. These microbes transform sugars and carbs into lactic acid, creating the tangy, acidic environment that keeps your food safe and delicious. They're the same friendly organisms that make yogurt creamy, sauerkraut crunchy, and kimchi lively. Without them, fermentation simply wouldn't happen.

Safety & Hygiene: 7 Practical Rules

Fermentation is natural, but it requires some care. Just follow these simple rules to ensure safety and great results:

1. Wash your hands thoroughly before starting.
2. Use clean tools, ideally glass, stainless steel, or wood.
3. Avoid plastic and reactive metals (copper, aluminum).
4. Keep ingredients submerged under brine: no oxygen = no mold.
5. Taste and check regularly—your nose and tongue are your best sensors.
6. Never use damaged or moldy ingredients.
7. If it smells bad or off, don't risk it: discard and start again.

Minimal Gear (+ Optional Upgrades)

You don't need fancy equipment to get started. The basics are enough:

- Glass jars with lids (repurposed canning jars work fine).
- Weights to keep food submerged (you can improvise with glass pebbles or water-filled bags).
- A spoon and a digital scale.

If you want to make the process easier and more controlled, consider optional upgrades:

- Airlocks to release gas while keeping oxygen out.
- Fermentation lids with seals.
- Ceramic or glass weights designed to fit jars.

With just the bare essentials, you can already ferment successfully. The upgrades are simply a step toward more convenience and precision.

UNITS OF MEASURE

US Customary vs. Metric (cups/tsp/Tbsp vs g/mL)

Many American recipes use cups, teaspoons (tsp), and tablespoons (Tbsp). They're convenient but imprecise: two hurried tablespoons of salt can differ drastically in weight. The metric system (grams and milliliters) is standard and universal. By weighing ingredients with a digital scale, you'll achieve consistent, reliable results—no matter who follows the recipe.

Why Grams for Salt and Brines

Salt is the single most critical element in fermentation: the right percentage ensures both safety and success. Measuring by volume (cups, spoons) can be off by as much as 30%. Measuring by grams guarantees precision and repeatability—you can make the same recipe over and over with identical results.

Quick US ↔ Metric Conversions & Scale Calibration

- 1 cup = ~240 mL
- 1 Tbsp = 15 mL
- 1 tsp = 5 mL
- 1 oz = 28 g
- 1 lb = 454 g

Tip: check your digital scale's calibration from time to time. Use a calibration weight (e.g., 100g) or, if you don't have one, a standard coin to make sure your scale reads accurately.

Worked Examples: 2% Salt

Dry-Salted Vegetables:

- Weigh the vegetables (e.g., 1,000 g cabbage). Calculate 2% salt = 20 g. Massage the salt directly into the veggies—the brine will form naturally.

Brined Vegetables:

- Decide the brine weight (e.g., 1,000 g = 1,000 mL water). Calculate 2% salt = 20 g, dissolve it in the water, then submerge the vegetables fully.

WHO SHOULD USE FERMENTED FOODS & WHY

Who Benefits (Digestion, Microbiome, Immunity, Energy)

Fermented foods are more than just a trend—they provide real, measurable benefits:

- **Digestion:** they help break down fibers and complex carbs, making foods easier to digest.
- **Microbiome:** they introduce diverse live bacteria that support gut balance.
- **Immunity:** a healthy gut microbiome is closely linked to a stronger immune system.
- **Energy:** better nutrient absorption can make you feel lighter, more energetic, and focused.

When to Introduce & Cautions (Pregnancy, Immunocompromised, Allergies/Intolerances)

Introduce fermented foods gradually, especially if you're new to them. Start with a teaspoon and slowly increase.

- **Pregnancy:** generally safe if prepared correctly, but it's always wise to consult your doctor.
- **Immunocompromised individuals:** should be cautious and seek medical advice before adding ferments.
- **Allergies/Intolerances:** choose ferments that match your dietary needs (soy-free, dairy-free, gluten-free options are available).

Weekly Integration: Frequency, Portions, Everyday Pairings

You don't need large amounts to enjoy the benefits:

- **Frequency:** 1–2 servings per day are enough.
- **Portions:** just 2–3 tablespoons of sauerkraut, kimchi, or kefir can make a difference.
- **Pairings:**
  - ✓ Add sauerkraut or kimchi as a side to your main dishes.
  - ✓ Enjoy fermented yogurt with fruit and grains for breakfast.
  - ✓ Stir a little miso into soups or dressings for added depth.

The key is consistency, not quantity: small daily servings are what create long-term benefits.

SUPERFOODS PREVIEW

What a "Superfood" Is

Superfood isn't a strict scientific category—it's a way to describe foods with an exceptionally high density of nutrients. These ingredients are rich in vitamins, minerals, antioxidants, and phytonutrients, often in greater amounts than everyday foods. Adding them to your diet can give an extra boost to energy, vitality, and natural defenses.

Ingredients to Try with Fermentation

Fermentation not only preserves these nutrients but can also make them more bioavailable. Some "superfoods" pair especially well with fermentation:

- Fresh turmeric → blended into kimchi or fermented chutneys.
- Ginger→ a classic for kombucha and other fizzy ferments.
- Black garlic → created through slow fermentation, loaded with antioxidants.
- Berries→ perfect for short ferments in sparkling drinks or preserves.
- Seaweeds (nori, wakame) → incorporated into miso or savory sauces.
- Chia or flax seeds → boosted with short ferments alongside fruit.

This is just a sneak peek: in the bonus section you'll find a curated set of recipes designed to maximize the nutritional power of fermented superfoods.

CHAPTER 1

USING FERMENTED FOODS IN EVERYDAY COOKING

1.1 EVERYDAY APPLICATIONS

1.1.1 BOWLS & SALADS • SANDWICHES/TOAST/BURGERS & TACOS • NOODLE/RICE BOWLS

Ferments fit effortlessly into daily meals—no complicated recipes required. Just one spoonful can turn a simple dish into something special:

- **Bowls & salads:** add sauerkraut or kimchi to a mixed salad or grain bowl for crunch, acidity, and freshness.
- **Sandwiches, toast, burgers & tacos:** swap out heavy condiments with ferments. A burger topped with kimchi instead of bottled sauce gains depth and bold character. A toast with avocado and sauerkraut becomes lighter and more nourishing.
- **Noodle or rice bowls:** pair ramen, soba, or stir-fried rice with fermented vegetables. Their acidity perfectly balances rich, savory flavors.

1.1.2 QUICK SAUCES & TOPPINGS • PAIRINGS WITH MEAT/FISH/VEGETABLE PROTEINS

Ferments are natural shortcuts for boosting flavor without extra work:

Quick sauces & toppings: whisk miso into a vinaigrette, use kefir instead of yogurt in a refreshing dip, or sprinkle chopped kimchi as a spicy topping. Done in seconds.

Pairings with meat, fish & veggie proteins:

- **Meat:** sauer kraut or kimchi cut through the richness of fatty cuts.
- **Fish:** fermented soy sauce or miso enhances the delicate taste of white fish.
- **Vegetables & plant proteins:** tempeh or natto can be combined with grains and veggies to add protein and a layer of complexity.

The principle is simple: don't change your cooking—enhance it. Small daily gestures with ferments bring variety, flavor, and nutrition to your table.

CHAPTER 2
FRIDGE VS PANTRY

2.1 REFRIGERATOR STORAGE: TYPICAL DURATIONS & QUALITY CUES

2.1 REFRIGERATOR STORAGE: TYPICAL DURATIONS & QUALITY CUES

The refrigerator is the safest place to keep live ferments. Cold temperatures slow down microbial activity, preserving flavor and texture.

- **Typical duration:** most ferments last 4 weeks to 6 months. Kimchi and sauerkraut can last even longer, with flavor continuing to evolve.
- **Quality cues:** Pleasant sour, fresh aroma. Natural color, though slight darkening is normal. Crunchy texture (for vegetables). If you notice foul odors, slimy textures, or colorful mold on the surface, it's best to discard.

2.2 PASTEURIZING/CANNING: PROS & CONS (IMPACT ON PROBIOTICS & FLAVOR)

SOME CHOOSE TO PASTEURIZE OR STERILIZE FERMENTS TO EXTEND SHELF LIFE OUTSIDE THE FRIDGE.

- **Pros:**
  - ✓ Extended food safety.
  - ✓ Room-temperature storage for months.
- **Cons:**
  - ✓ Pasteurization kills live probiotics.
  - ✓ Flavor loses brightness and freshness.
  - ✓ Texture becomes more uniform, less crisp.

In short: if you want probiotic benefits, keep it unpasteurized. If convenience and long shelf life matter most, pasteurization is a practical option.

2.3 SPACE MANAGEMENT: SLIM CONTAINERS, LABELS, ROTATION

Fridge space is precious, but smart organization helps:

- **Slim containers:** use tall, narrow jars to maximize shelf space.
- **Clear labels:** always mark the date and contents (a marker on the lid works fine).
- **Rotation:** place newer jars in the back and use older ones first.

With a few simple habits, you'll always have fresh, safe, and easy-to-find ferments.

CHAPTER 3

INDEXES & TOOLS

3.1 INGREDIENTINDEX

A quick reference to locate recipes by main ingredient. Whether you've got cabbage, carrots, or fresh ginger on hand, this index points you straight to the right recipes without flipping through the whole book.

3.2 NEEDS INDEX (CRUNCHY, SPICY, SWEET, EVERYDAY USE)

Sometimes you choose based on what you're craving:

Crunchy: ferments that keep a crisp bite, like cucumbers and carrots.

Spicy: bold kimchi and fiery chutneys.

Sweet: fruit-forward kombucha or kefir.

Everyday use: basic sauerkraut, miso, soy sauce.

A sensory and functional index to simplify your choices.

3.3 SEASONAL PLANNER (GARDEN & MARKET)

Fermentation works best with seasonal rhythms.This planner highlights what's abundant and affordable throughout the year:

- **Spring:** asparagus, radishes, fresh herbs.
- **Summer:** tomatoes, cucumbers, berries.
- **Fall:** cabbages, pumpkins, apples.
- **Winter:** root vegetables, green cabbage, citrus.

Plan smarter, ferment fresher, eat sustainably.

3.4 PHOTOCOPIABLE BATCH SHEETS (SMALL-BATCH / FAMILY)

Ready-to-use templates for tracking quantities, timelines, and outcomes:

- **Small-Batch format:** great for quick tests and small runs.
- **Family format:** :designed for larger batches and shared meals.

These sheets help you stay organized, compare experiments, and easily replicate your favorites.

3.5 RESOURCES & FURTHER READING

For readers who want to go deeper:

- Key books on traditional and modern fermentation.
- Trusted websites and online communities of fermenters.
- Digital tools and apps for recipe logging and planning.

CHAPTER 4 BRINED VEGETABLES (32 RECIPES)

4.1 METHODS & STEP-BY-STEP PROCEDURES

4.1.1 PRODUCE SELECTION, CUTS, BRINE %, WEIGHTS, BURPING, TEMPERATURE

Brined vegetable fermentation is one of the easiest and safest methods. For reliable results:

- **Produce selection:** use fresh vegetables without bruises or mold. Cucumbers, carrots, cauliflower, radishes, and green beans are excellent choices.
- **Cuts**: keep pieces uniform (sticks, slices, florets) for even fermentation.
- **Brine %:** the standard is 2–3% salt relative to the weight of the water (e.g., 20–30 g salt per 1 L water ≈ 0.7–1 oz salt per 34 fl oz water).
- **Weights:** ensure vegetables remain fully submerged with glass/ceramic weights or improvised solutions (like a water-filled bag). For example, if fermenting 1,000 g (2.2 lb) of vegetables in 1 L (34 fl oz) brine, use a weight heavy enough to keep everything below the liquid.
- **Burping:** during the first few days, fermentation produces gas. If you're not using an airlock, slightly open the jar once daily to release pressure.
- **Temperature:** the sweet spot is 64–72 °F (18–22 °C). Higher temps speed up fermentation but may soften texture.

4.1.2 VISUAL/AROMA CUES: NORMAL VS NOT NORMAL

LEARNING WHAT'S NORMAL BUILDS CONFIDENCE AND SAFETY:

- **Normal:**
  Visible bubbles. Cloudy brine.
  Pleasant sour, fresh aroma.
  Slight color change.
- **Not normal:**
  Colored mold (green, black, pink).
  Rotten or putrid smell.
  Slimy texture or vegetables floating above the brine.

When in doubt, throw it out. The golden rule: trust your eyes and nose.

4.2.1 CUCUMBERS (6 RECIPES)

Basic equipment for all recipes: 2 L (≈2 qt) jar for~1,000g (2.2lb) cucumbers, or multiple smaller jars; fermentation weights; long spoon; digital scale; optional airlock lid.

Headspace: leave 2–3 cm (¾–1 in).

Crispness tip: trim off the blossom end of each cucumber (1–2 mm) before fermenting.

1) GARLIC-DILL SPEARS

Step-by-Step:

1. **Prep cucumbers:** wash, trim blossom ends (1–2 mm), cut into even spears.
2. **Jar ready:** clean and dry the 2 L (≈2 qt) jar.
3. **Make brine:** dissolve 25 g (0.9 oz) salt in 1,000 mL (34 fl oz) room-temp water.
4. **Layer aromatics:** 2 dill sprigs + 2 garlic cloves at the bottom.
5. **Pack:** insert spears tightly; add remaining dill and garlic on top.
6. **Pour brine:** fully cover; keep 2–3 cm (¾–1 in) headspace. Make extra 2.5% brine if needed.
7. **De-bubble + weight:** release trapped air; place weight to keep everything below the brine.
8. **Ferment:** 7–10 days at 64–72 °F (18–22 °C); burp daily if no airlock.
9. **Monitor:** bubbles + slight cloudiness = normal. Start tasting on day 7.
10. **Refrigerate when flavor is right;** keeps 4–8 weeks (or longer), flavor evolves.

Ingredients:

- **Cucumbers:** 1,000 g (2.2 lb), cut into spears
- **Garlic**: 4 cloves, lightly crushed Fresh dill: 4 sprigs
- **Brine**: 1,000 mL (34 fl oz) water + 25 g (0.9 oz) salt (2.5%)

Recommended Method:

- **Standard (room temp):** best choice for this recipe. Keep out of the fridge at 64–72 °F (18–22 °C) for 7–10 days → fuller garlic–dill expression and great crunch.
- **If it's hot indoors (>75–77 °F / 24–25 °C):** choose hybrid → start 12–24 h at room temp, then finish in the fridge (1–2 weeks) for extra crispness.
- **Cold-ferment (all in fridge):** maximum crunch; allow 2–3+ weeks, milder flavor.

2)NEW YORK HALF-SOUR

Ingredients

- **Small wholecucumbers:** 1,000g(2.2lb)
- **Garlic:** 3 cloves
- **Dill seeds:** 1–2 tsp
- **Black peppercorns:** 5
- Brine: 1,000mL(34floz)water + 20 g (0.7 oz) salt (2%)

Garlic: 3 cloves **Dill seeds:** 1–2 tsp **Black peppercorns:**

Step-by-Step

1. Wash, trim blossom ends (1–2 mm), keep cucumbers whole.
2. Clean 2 L (≈2 qt) jar.
3. Brine: dissolve 20 g (0.7 oz) salt in 1,000 mL (34 fl oz) water.
4. Bottom layer: garlic, dill seeds, peppercorns.
5. Pack cucumbers very tightly.
6. Cover with brine; 2–3 cm (¾–1 in) headspace.
7. De-bubble; add weight.
8. Ferment 3–5 days at 64–72 °F (18–22 °C); burp if needed.
9. Half-sour = fresh, light flavor; start tasting on day 3.
10. Refrigerate when ready; best within 2–3 weeks.

Recommended Method

- **Standard (room temp):** ideal for classic half-sour: 3–5 days at 64–72 °F (18–22 °C) → bright, fresh, lightly tangy.
- **Hybrid (hot weather):** 12–24 h at room temp, then fridge to finish (total 5–10 days). Preserves that fresh snap.
- **Cold-ferment:** all in the fridge 2–3 weeks for very gentle sourness and excellent crunch.

3)WHOLE DILL CLASSICS

Ingredients

- **Small whole cucumbers**: 1,200 g (2.6 lb)

  Fresh dill: 6 sprigs
- **Garlic:** 4 cloves
- **Bay leaves:** 2

  Brine: 1,000 mL (34 fl oz) water + 30 g (1.0
- oz) salt (3%)

Step-by-Step

1. Prep cucumbers (wash, trim blossom ends). Keep them whole.
2. Use a larger vessel: 3 L (≈3 qt) jar recommended.
3. Brine 3%: dissolve 30 g (1.0 oz) salt in 1,000 mL (34 fl oz) water.
4. Bottom: half the dill + half the garlic + 1 bay leaf.
5. Pack cucumbers tightly; add remaining dill, garlic, bay on top.
6. Pour brine to cover; add extra 3% brine if needed; 2–3 cm (¾–1 in) headspace.
7. De-bubble; weight on top.
8. Ferment 10–14 days at 64–68 °F (18–20 °C) for cleaner flavor and better crunch.
9. Taste from day 10; continue if you prefer bolder sourness.
10. Refrigerate; keeps 6–8 weeks (or longer), flavor keeps maturing.

Recommended Method

- **Standard (cool room temp):** recommended at 64–68 °F (18–20 °C) for 10–14 days. Lower room temps help preserve crunch in whole cucumbers.
- **Hybrid (hot weather):** start 12–24 h at room temp, then fridge for a slow finish (2–3 weeks total) → very crisp, controlled acidity.
- **Cold-ferment:** all in the fridge 3–4+ weeks for maximum crunch and a super clean profile.

4) SPICY JALAPEÑO SPEARS

Ingredients

- **Cucumber spears:** 1,000 g (2.2 lb)
- **Jalapeños:** 2, sliced (include seeds for more heat)
- **Garlic:** 3 cloves
- **Coriander seeds:** 1–2 tsp
- **Dried chili:** to taste
- **Brine:** 1,000 mL (34 fl oz) water + 25 g (0.9 oz) salt (2.5%)

Recommended Method

- **Standard (room temp):** preferred for full spice expression in 7–9 days at 64–72 °F (18–22 °C).
- **Hybrid (hot weather):** 12–24 h room temp, then fridge 1–2 weeks → crisper spears, cleaner chili notes.
- **Cold-ferment:** all in fridge 2–3+ weeks for softer heat and very firm texture.

Step-by-Step

1. Prep cucumber spears; slice jalapeños.
2. Clean 2 L (≈2 qt) jar.
3. Brine 2.5%: 25 g (0.9 oz) salt / 1,000 mL (34 fl oz) water.
4. Bottom aromatics: garlic + coriander + a pinch of dried chili.
5. Pack spears and jalapeños in alternating layers for even heat.
6. Add brine; 2–3 cm (¾–1 in) headspace.
7. De-bubble; add weight.
8. Ferment 7–9 days at 64–72 °F (18–22 °C); burp if needed.
9. Taste from day 7; extend for more heat and tang.
10. Refrigerate; best within 4–6 weeks.

5) MUSTARD SEED & BAY

Ingredients

- **Cucumbers, sliced into rounds:** 1,000 g (2.2 lb)
- **Mustard seeds:** 2 Tbsp
- **Bay leaves:** 2
- **Garlic:** 2 cloves
- **Brine:** 1,000 mL (34 fl oz) water + 25 g (0.9 oz) salt (2.5%)

Step-by-Step

1. Slice rounds evenly (0.5–1 cm / ¼–⅜ in).
2. Clean 2 L (≈2 qt) jar.
3. Brine 2.5%: 25 g (0.9 oz) salt / 1,000 mL (34 fl oz) water.
4. Bottom: 1 Tbsp mustard + 1 bay + 1 garlic.
5. Pack cucumber rounds; add remaining mustard, bay, garlic on top.
6. Cover with brine; 2–3 cm (¾–1 in) headspace.
7. De-bubble; weight on top.
8. Ferment 8–10 days at 64–72 °F (18–22 °C).
9. Taste from day 8 for aromatic, gently spicy notes.
10. Refrigerate; enjoy within 4–6 weeks.

Recommended Method

- **Standard (room temp):** recommended to draw out spicy–aromatic notes in 8–10 days at 64–72 °F (18–22 °C).
- **Hybrid (hot weather):** 12–24 h at room temp, then fridge for 1–2 weeks → superior crunch in slices.
- **Cold-ferment:** all in fridge 2–3+ weeks for softer spice and compact texture.

6) HERB-GARDEN CUCUMBERS

Ingredients

- **Cucumbers, halved or speared:** 1,000 g (2.2 lb)
- **Mixed fresh herbs:** basil, thyme, oregano (1 small bunch total)
- **Garlic:** 2 cloves
- **Brine:** 1,000 mL (34 fl oz) water + 25 g (0.9 oz) salt (2.5%)

Step-by-Step

1. Prep cucumbers (wash, trim blossom ends), cut in halves/spears.
2. Clean 2 L (≈2 qt) jar.
3. Brine 2.5%: 25 g (0.9 oz) salt / 1,000 mL (34 fl oz) water.
4. Bottom: half the herbs + 1 garlic clove.
5. Pack cucumbers; top with remaining herbs + 1 garlic.
6. Add brine; 2–3 cm (¾–1 in) headspace.
7. De-bubble; add weight.
8. Ferment 6–8 days at 64–72 °F (18–22 °C).
9. Taste from day 6; expect a bright, herbal profile.
10. Refrigerate; ideal within 4–5 weeks.

Recommended Method

- **Standard (room temp):** best to showcase fresh herbs in 6–8 days at 64–72 °F (18–22 °C).
- **Hybrid (hot weather):** 12–24 h at room temp, then fridge (1–2 weeks) → brighter herbs, greener color.
- **Cold-ferment:** all in fridge 2–3 weeks for a very gentle herbal profile.

4.2 RECIPE SECTION (32)

4.2.2 CARROTS (4 RECIPES)

Basic equipment for all recipes:2 L (≈2qt) jarfor ~1,000g(2.2lb)carrots;fermentation weights; long spoon; digital scale; optional airlock lid.

Headspace: leave 2–3 cm (¾–1 in).

Crispness tip: choose firm, fresh carrots; make uniform cuts. Optional: ice-water soak 10–15 min, then dry before packing.

1)GINGER CARROT STICKS

Ingredients

- **Carrots, cut into sticks:** 1,000 g (2.2 lb)
- **Fresh ginger, matchsticks:** 20–30 g (0.7–1.1 oz)
- **Garlic:** 2 cloves (crushed)
- **Coriander seeds:** 1 tsp (optional)
- **Brine:** 1,000 mL (34 fl oz) water + 25 g (0.9 oz) salt (2.5%)

Step-by-Step

1. Prep carrots: peel if needed; cut even sticks (≈1×1×8–10 cm / ⅜×⅜×3–4 in).
2. Jar: clean and dry 2 L (≈2 qt) jar.
3. Brine: dissolve 25 g (0.9 oz) salt in 1,000 mL (34 fl oz) room-temp water.
4. Aromatics: add ginger, garlic, coriander to the bottom.
5. Pack: arrange sticks upright, snug.
6. Cover with brine: keep 2–3 cm (¾–1 in) headspace.
7. De-bubble and weight to keep all below brine.
8. Ferment: 6–8 days at 64–72 °F (18–22 °C); burp if no airlock.
9. Taste from day 6; cloudiness/bubbles are normal.
10. Refrigerate when ready; use within 4–6 weeks.

Recommended Method

- **Standard(roomtemp):**recommended to draw out spicy–aromatic notes in 8–10 days at 64–72 °F (18–22 °C).
- **Hybrid (hot weather):** 12–24 h at room temp, then fridge for 1–2 weeks → superior crunch in slices.
- **Cold-ferment**: all in fridge 2–3+ weeks for softer spice and compact texture.

2) HERBED CARROT COINS

Ingredients

- **Carrots, sliced rounds (0.5–1 cm / ¼–⅜ in):** 1,000 g (2.2 lb)
- **Mixed fresh herbs (parsley, dill, thyme):** 10 g (0.35 oz) total
- **Garlic:** 2 cloves
- **Brine:** 1,000 mL (34 fl oz) water + 25 g (0.9 oz) salt (2.5%)

Step-by-Step

1. Slice carrots evenly; roughly chop herbs.
2. Clean 2 L (≈2 qt) jar.
3. Brine 2.5% as above.
4. Bottom: half the herbs + 1 garlic clove.
5. Pack rounds; top with remaining herbs + 1 garlic clove.
6. Add brine; 2–3 cm (¾–1 in) headspace.
7. De-bubble; place weight.
8. Ferment 7–9 days at 64–72 °F (18–22 °C).
9. Taste from day 7 for bright acidity and herbal notes.
10. Refrigerate; best within 4–6 weeks.

Recommended Method

- **Standard (room temp):** 7–9 days at 64–72 °F (18–22 °C) to highlight fresh herb aromas.
- **Hybrid (hot weather):** 12–24 h at room temp, then fridge 1–2 weeks → greener color, top crunch.
- **Cold-ferment:** 2–3 weeks in fridge for very gentle herbal notes.

3) CURRY CARROTS

Step-by-Step

1. Prep carrots (uniform sticks/rounds).
2. Clean 2 L (≈2 qt) jar.
3. Whisk curry into a cup of the brine, then combine with the rest (prevents floating clumps).
4. Bottom: mustard seeds + garlic.
5. Pack carrots; pour curry brine; 2–3 cm (¾–1 in) headspace.
6. De-bubble; add weight.
7. Ferment 7–10 days at 64–72 °F (18–22 °C); burp if needed.
8. Taste from day 7; yellow color is normal.
9. Extend 1–2 days for stronger spice.
10. Refrigerate; enjoy within 4–6 weeks.

Ingredients

Carrots,sticks or rounds: 1,000 g (2.2 lb)

Curry powder: 1–2 Tbsp (to taste)

Mustard seeds: 1 tsp

Garlic: 2 cloves

Brine: 1,000 mL (34 fl oz) water + 25 g (0.9 oz) salt (2.5%)

Recommended Method

- **Standard(coolroomtemp):** recommended at 64–68 °F (18–20 °C) for 10–14 days. Lower room temps help preserve crunch in whole cucumbers.
- **Hybrid (hot weather):** start 12–24 h at room temp, then fridge for a slow finish (2–3 weeks total) → very crisp, controlled acidity.
- **Cold-ferment:** all in the fridge 3–4+ weeks for maximum crunch and a super clean profile.

4) LEMON-PEPPER CARROTS

Ingredients

- **Carrots, sticks or rounds:** 1,000 g (2.2 lb)
- **Lemon zest strips (no pith):** from 1 lemon
- **Black peppercorns:** 10
- **Bay leaf:** 1 (optional)
- **Garlic:** 1 clove
- **Brine:** 1,000 mL (34 fl oz) water + 25 g (0.9 oz) salt (2.5%)

Step-by-Step

1. Prep carrots; peel lemon zest into strips.
2. Clean 2 L (≈2 qt) jar.
3. Brine 2.5% as above.
4. Bottom: half the zest, half the peppercorns, bay, garlic.
5. Pack carrots; top with remaining zest and peppercorns.
6. Add brine; 2–3 cm (¾–1 in) headspace.
7. De-bubble; add weight.
8. Ferment 6–8 days at 64–72 °F (18–22 °C).
9. Taste from day 6 for bright citrus and balanced pepper.
10. Refrigerate; ideal within 4–5 weeks.

Recommended Method

- **Standard (room temp):** 6–8 days at 64–72 °F (18–22 °C) for crisp citrus and balanced pepper.
- **Hybrid (hot weather):** 12–24 h room temp, then fridge 1–2 weeks → fresher citrus, extra crunch.
- **Cold-ferment:** 2–3 weeks in fridge for gentle citrus and maximum crunch.

4.2.3 RADISHES & DAIKON (4 RECIPES)

Basic equipment for all recipes: 2 L (≈2 qt) jar for ~1,000 g (2.2 lb); fermentation weights; long spoon; digital scale; optional airlock lid.

Headspace: leave 2–3 cm (¾–1 in).

Crispness tip: choose firm, fresh carrots; make uniform cuts. Optional: ice-water soak 10–Crispness & color notes: choose firm radishes and very fresh daikon; keep cuts uniform. Red radishes will turn the brine pink—that's normal. A sulfurous aroma during active ferment is also normal.
15 min, then dry before packing.

1) PINK RADISH COINS

Recommended Method

- **Standard (cool room):** 4–6 days at 64–68 °F (18–20 °C) for bright color and crunch.
- **Hybrid (hot weather):** 12–24 h at room temp, then fridge 1–2 weeks → vivid color, extra crispness.
- **Cold-ferment:** all in fridge 2–3 weeks for gentle acidity and very firm texture.

Ingredients

- **Red radishes, sliced rounds (0.5–1 cm / ¼–⅜ in):** 1,000 g (2.2 lb)
- **White peppercorns:** 10
- **Garlic: 1** clove (optional)
- **Brine:** 1,000mL(34floz)water+25g(0.9 oz) salt (2.5%)

Step-by-Step

1. Prepradishes: trim tops/roots, wash, slice evenly.
2. Jar: clean and dry (2 L / ≈2 qt).
3. Brine 2.5%: dissolve 25 g (0.9 oz) salt in 1,000 mL (34 fl oz) room-temp water.
4. Aromatics: pepper (and garlic if using) on the bottom.
5. Pack the rounds snugly.
6. Cover with brine; keep 2–3 cm (¾–1 in) headspace.
7. De-bubble and weight to keep all below brine.
8. Ferment4–6 days at 64–68 °F (18–20 °C); burp if no airlock.
9. Taste from day 4; pink brine and strong aroma are normal.
10. Refrigerate when ready; best within 3–4 weeks.

2) CHILI DAIKON MATCHSTICKS

Ingredients

- **Daikon, cut into matchsticks:** 1,000 g (2.2 lb)
- **Chili flakes or gochugaru:** 1–2 Tbsp (to taste)
- **Fresh ginger, matchsticks:** 10–15 g (0.35–0.5 oz)
- **Garlic:** 2 cloves
- **Brine:** 1,000 mL (34 fl oz) water + 25 g (0.9 oz) salt (2.5%)

Step-by-Step

1. Cut daikon into even matchsticks.
2. Jar: clean 2 L (≈2 qt).
3. Make brine 2.5% as above.
4. Bottom layer: ginger + garlic; add chili.
5. Pack daikon; distribute spices evenly.
6. Add brine; 2–3 cm (¾–1 in) headspace.
7. De-bubble; weight on top.
8. Ferment5–7 days at 64–72 °F (18–22 °C).
9. Taste from day 5; light cloudiness is normal.
10. Refrigerate; enjoy within 4–6 weeks

Recommended Method

- **Standard (room temp):** 5–7 days at 64–72 °F (18–22 °C) for full spice and good crunch.
- **Hybrid (hot weather):** 12–24 h room temp, then fridge 1–2 weeks → cleaner spice, firmer bite.
- **Cold-ferment:** 2–3+ weeks in fridge for milder heat and maximum crispness.

3) WATERMELON RADISH & ORANGE ZEST

Ingredients

- **Watermelon radish, sliced rounds (0.5–1 cm / ¼–⅜ in):** 1,000 g (2.2 lb)
- **Orange zest strips (no pith):** from 1 orange
- **Pink peppercorns:** 1tsp
- **Brine:** 1,000mL(34floz)water+25g(0.9oz) salt (2.5%)

Recommended Method

- **Standard(roomtemp):** 5–7 days at 64–72 °F (18–22 °C) for full spice and good crunch.
- **Hybrid (hot weather):** 12–24 h room temp, then fridge 1–2 weeks → cleaner spice, firmer bite.
- **Cold-ferment:** 2–3+ weeks in fridge for milder heat and maximum crispness.

Step-by-Step

1.Slicewatermelon radish into even rounds.

2.Jar: clean 2 L (≈2 qt). 3.Brine 2.5% as above. 4.Bottom: half the zest + pink peppercorns. 5.Pack rounds; top with remaining zest. 6.Add brine; 2–3 cm (¾–1 in) headspace. 7.De-bubble; weight on top. 8.Ferment5–7 days at 64–68 °F (18–20 °C).

9.Taste from day 5; expect bright citrus and fresh tang.

10.Refrigerate; best within 4–5 weeks.

4) RADISH & SPRING ONION

Ingredients

- **Mixed radishes (red/pink), wedges or rounds:** 800 g (1.76 lb)
- **Spring onions (white & green), thin rings:** 200 g (0.44 lb)
- **Garlic:** 1 clove (optional)
  Mustard seeds: 1 tsp (optional)
- **Brine:** 1,000 mL (34 fl oz) water + 25 g (0.9 oz) salt (2.5%)
-

Step-by-Step

1.Prep radishes and spring onions into even cuts. 2.Jar: clean 2 L (≈2 qt). 3.Brine 2.5% as above. 4.Bottom: garlic (optional) + mustard seeds. 5.Pack radishes and spring onions in alternating layers. 6.Cover with brine; 2–3 cm (¾–1 in) headspace. 7.De-bubble; weight to submerge. 8.Ferment4–6 days at 64–68 °F (18–20 °C) (spring onions ferment fast).

9.Taste from day 4; vegetal aroma is normal.

10.Refrigerate; best within3–4 weeks.

Recommended Method

- **Standard (cool room):** 4–6 days at 64–68 °F (18–20 °C) to keep onion intensity in check and preserve crunch.
- **Hybrid (hot weather):** 12–24 h room temp, then fridge 1–2 weeks → cleaner profle, brighter color.
- **Cold-ferment:** 2–3 weeks in fridge for gentle flavor and very firm structure.

4.2 RECIPE SECTION (32)

4.2.4 CAULIFLOWER&BRASSICAS(4 RECIPES)

Basic equipmentforallrecipes:2 L(≈2 qt)jar for~1,000g(2.2lb);fermentation weights; long spoon; digital scale; optional airlock lid.

Headspace: leave 2–3 cm (¾–1 in).

Brassica notes: a sulfurous aroma early on is normal; for crisp texture, favor cooler rooms (64–68 °F / 18–20 °C) and uniform floret cuts.

1) TURMERIC CAULIFLOWER

Ingredients

- **Cauliflower, florets:** 1,000 g (2.2 lb)
- Fresh turmeric, matchsticks 20 g (0.7 oz) or turmeric powder 1–2 tsp
- **Black peppercorns:** ½–1tsp (optional, **supports bioavailability)**
- **Garlic:** 2 cloves
- **Brine:** 1,000 mL(34floz)water + 25 g (0.9 oz) salt (2.5%)

Step-by-Step

1.Slice watermelon radish into even rounds. 2.Jar: clean 2 L (≈2 qt). 3.Brine 2.5% as above. 4.Bottom: half the zest + pink peppercorns. 5.Pack rounds; top with remaining zest. 6.Add brine; 2–3 cm (¾–1 in) headspace. 7.De-bubble; weight on top. 8.Ferment5–7 days at 64–68 °F (18–20 °C). 9.Taste from day 5; expect bright citrus and fresh tang.

10.Refrigerate; best within 4–5 weeks.

Recommended Method

- **Standard (cool room):** 7–10 days at 64–68 °F (18–20 °C) for crisp florets and balanced spice.
- **Hybrid (hot weather):** 12–24 h room temp, then fridge 1–2 weeks → clean profile, firm texture.
- **Cold-ferment:** all in fridge 2–3+ weeks for gentler flavor and maximum crunch.

2) ROMANESCO & GARLIC

Ingredients

- **Romanesco, florets:** 1,000 g (2.2 lb)
- **Garlic:** 4 cloves
- **Black peppercorns:** 1tsp
- **Bay leaf:** 1 (optional)
- **Brine:** 1,000mL(34floz) water + 25 g (0.9 oz) salt (2.5%)

Step-by-Step

1.Cut into even florets (2–3 cm / ¾–1¼ in). 2.Jar: clean 2 L (≈2 qt). 3.Brine 2.5% as above. 4.Bottom: garlic, pepper (and bay). 5.Pack florets; avoid over-compacting. 6.Add brine; 2–3 cm (¾–1 in) headspace. 7.De-bubble; weight on top. 8.Ferment6–8 days at 64–68 °F (18–20 °C). 9.Taste from day 6; expect a bold yet fresh aroma.

10.Refrigerate; enjoy within 4–5 weeks.

Recommended Method

- **Standard (cool room):** 6–8 days at 64–68 °F (18–20 °C) for clean flavor and crunch. **Hybrid (hot weather):** 12–24 h room temp, then fridge 1–2 weeks → composed acidity, firm bite. **Cold-ferment:** 2–3 weeks in fridge for a gentler profile. **Hybrid (hot weather):** 12–24 h at room temp, then fridge for 1–2 weeks → superior crunch in slices. **Cold-ferment:** all in fridge 2–3+ weeks for softer spice and compact texture.

3) CAULI-CARROT GIARDINIERA

Ingredients

- **Cauliflower, florets** 600 g(1.32lb)
- **Carrots, sliced rounds:**400 g (0.88 lb)
- **Mustard seeds:** 1 tsp
- **Dried oregano: 1 tsp**
- **Garlic:** 2 cloves
- **Chili flakes:** totaste
- **Brine:** 1,000 mL(34floz) water + 25 g (0.9 oz) salt (2.5%)

Step-by-Step

1.Prep cauliflower (even florets) and carrots (0.5–1 cm / ¼–⅜ in rounds).

2.Jar: clean 2 L (≈2 qt). 3.Brine 2.5% as above. 4.Bottom: mustard, oregano, garlic, chili. 5.Pack alternating layers to distribute density and aromatics.

6.Add brine; 2–3 cm (¾–1 in) headspace.

7.De-bubble; weight on top.

8.Ferment7–9 days at 64–68 °F (18–20 °C).

9.Taste from day 7; herbal, lightly spicy.

10.Refrigerate; best within 4–6 weeks.

Recommended Method

- **Standard (cool room):** 7–9 days at 64–68 °F (18–20 °C) for balance of crunch and aromatics.
- **Hybrid (hot weather)**: 12–24 h room temp, then fridge 1–2 weeks → brighter colors, firmer texture.
- **Cold-ferment:** 2–3 weeks in fridge for a gentler profile.

4) BROCCOLI STEM COINS

Ingredients

- **Broccolistems peeled, sliced rounds (0.5–1 cm / ¼–⅜ in):** 1,000 g (2.2 lb)
- **Lemon zest strips:** from 1 lemon
- **Garlic:** 1 clove
- **Chili flakes:** ½–1 tsp (optional)
- **Brine:** 1,000 mL (34 fl oz) water + 30 g (1.0 oz) salt (3%) → supports firmness

Step-by-Step

1. Peel stems (remove fibrous outer layer) and slice evenly.
2. Jar: clean 2 L (≈2 qt).
3. Brine 3%: dissolve 30 g (1.0 oz) salt in 1,000 mL (34 fl oz) water.
4. Bottom: lemon zest, garlic, chili.
5. Pack rounds; don't over-compress.
6. Add brine; 2–3 cm (¾–1 in) headspace.
7. De-bubble; weight to submerge.
8. Ferment4–6 days at 64–68 °F (18–20 °C).
9. Taste from day 4; bright citrus, gentle heat.
10. Refrigerate; best within 3–4 weeks.

Recommended Method

- **Standard (cool room):** 4–6 days at 64–68 °F (18–20 °C) for maximum firmness.
- **Hybrid (hot weather):** 12–24 h room temp, then fridge 1–2 weeks → extra crunch.
- **Cold-ferment:** 2–3 weeks in fridge for delicate flavor and compact texture.

4.2 RECIPE SECTION (32)

4.2.5 GREEN BEANS & SNOW PEAS (3 RECIPES)

Basic equipment for all recipes: 2 L (≈2 qt) jar for ~1,000 g (2.2 lb) batches; fermentation weights; long spoon; digital scale; optional airlock lid.

Headspace: leave 2–3 cm (¾–1 in).

Crispness tips: choose young, firm beans (trim ends), keep uniform lengths; optional ice-water soak 10–15 min, then dry.

1) DILLY BEANS

Ingredients

- **Green beans, whole or cut:** 1,000 g (2.2 lb)
- **Fresh dill:** 6 sprigs
  Garlic: 3 cloves
- **Black peppercorns:** 1 tsp (≈ 2 g / 0.07 oz)
- **(Optional) Mustard seeds:** 1 tsp
- **Brine:** 1,000 mL (34 fl oz) water + 30 g (1.0 oz) salt (3%)
-

Step-by-Step

1. Trim ends; leave beans whole or cut into 2.5 in (6–7 cm) pieces.
2. Jar: clean and dry (2 L / ≈2 qt).
3. Brine 3%: dissolve 30 g (1.0 oz) salt in 1,000 mL (34 fl oz) water.
4. Bottom layer: half the dill, garlic, pepper (and mustard).
5. Pack beans upright and tight; top with remaining dill.
6. Cover with brine; keep 2–3 cm (¾–1 in) headspace.
7. De-bubble; place weight to keep all submerged.
8. Ferment6–8 days at 64–68 °F (18–20 °C); burp if no airlock.
9. Taste from day 6 for bright tang and crunch.
10. Refrigerate; best within 4–6 weeks.

Recommended Method

- **Standard (cool room):** 6–8 days at 64–68 °F (18–20 °C) → optimal crunch, clean dill-garlic profile.
- **Hybrid (hot weather):** 12–24 h room temp, then fridge 1–2 weeks → firmer beans, composed acidity.
- **Cold-ferment:** all in fridge 2–3+ weeks for milder flavor and maximum crunch.
- **Snow peas variation:** replace some/all beans; shorten to 3–5 days at 64–68 °F (18–20 °C) (or cold-ferment 1–2 weeks). Optionally use 2.5% brine (25 g / 0.9 oz salt per 1,000 mL / 34 fl oz water) for a gentler profile.

2) GARLICKY GREEN BEANS

Ingredients

- **Green beans, whole:** 1,000 g (2.2 lb)
- **Garlic:** 6 cloves (lightly crushed)
- **Bay leaf:** 1
- **Red chili flakes:** ½–1 tsp (optional)
- **Brine:** 1,000 mL (34 fl oz) water + 30 g (1.0 oz) salt (3%)

Step-by-Step

1. Prep beans (trim ends).
2. Jar: clean 2 L (≈2 qt).
3. Brine 3% as above.
4. Bottom: half the garlic + bay (+ chili if using).
5. Pack beans upright and snug.
6. Add brine; 2–3 cm (¾–1 in) headspace.
7. De-bubble; add weight.
8. Ferment6–8 days at 64–68 °F (18–20 °C).
9. Taste from day 6; bold but fresh garlic aroma is normal.
10. Refrigerate; enjoy within 4–6 weeks.

Recommended Method

- **Standard (cool room):** 6–8 days at 64–68 °F (18–20 °C) → expressive garlic, crisp beans.
- **Hybrid (hot weather):** 12–24 h room temp, then fridge 1–2 weeks → cleaner profile, very firm texture.
- **Cold-ferment: 2**–3 weeks in fridge for gentle flavor and maximum crunch.
- **Snow peas variation:** 3–5 days at 64–68 °F (18–20 °C) (or cold-ferment 1–2 weeks); optional 2.5% brine for delicacy.

3) SPICY SESAME BEANS

Ingredients

- G**reenbeans, whole or cut:** 1,000 g (2.2 lb)
- **Chili flakes or gochugaru:** 1–2 Tbsp (to taste)
- **Garlic:** 3 cloves
- **Fresh ginger, matchsticks:** 10 g (0.35 oz) (optional)
- **Toasted sesame seeds**: 2 tsp (note: no oil in brine; add sesame oil only when serving)
- **Brine:** 1,000 mL (34 fl oz) water + 30 g (1.0 oz) salt (3%)

Step-by-Step

1. Trim beans; cut if needed.
2. Jar: clean 2 L (≈2 qt).
3. Brine 3% as above.
4. Bottom aromatics: garlic + ginger + chili + 1 tsp sesame seeds.
5. Pack beans; distribute spices evenly.
6. Add brine; 2–3 cm (¾–1 in) headspace.
7. De-bubble; add weight.
8. Ferment6–8 days at 64–68 °F (18–20 °C).
9. Taste from day 6; gradual heat build is normal.
10. Refrigerate; at serving, add a dash of sesame oil and the remaining 1 tsp toasted seeds. Best within 4–6 weeks.

Recommended Method

- **Standard (cool room):** 6–8 days at 64–68 °F (18–20 °C) → full spice, firm beans.
- **Hybrid (hot weather):** 12–24 h room temp, then fridge 1–2 weeks → cleaner chili notes, superior crunch.
- **Cold-ferment:** 2–3+ weeks in fridge for softer heat and very firm texture.
- **Snow peas variation:** 3–5 days at 64–68 °F (18–20 °C) (or cold-ferment 1–2 weeks); optional 2.5% brine for a lighter touch.

4.2.6 PEPPERS (3 RECIPES)

Basic equipment for allrecipes: 2 L(≈2qt)jarfor~1,000g(2.2lb);fermentation weights; long spoon; digital scale; optional airlock lid.

Headspace: leave 2–3 cm (¾–1 in).

Floating note: peppers tend to float — pack tightly, use weights and optionally a cabbage-leaf or silicone cap.

Crispness & color: favor cool rooms (64–68 °F / 18–20 °C) to keep bright colors and good bite.

1) SWEET BELL STRIPS

Ingredients

- **Sweet bell peppers (red/yellow), sliced into strips:** 1,000 g (2.2 lb)
- **Garlic:** 3 cloves, crushed
- **Dried oregano:** 1–2 tsp
- **Black peppercorns:** 1tsp
- **(Optional) Bay leaf:** 1
- **Brine:** 1,000 mL(34floz)water+25 g (0.9 oz) salt (2.5%)

Step-by-Step

1. Prep peppers: remove stems, seeds, membranes; cut even strips (1–2 cm / ⅜–¾ in).
2. Jar: clean and dry (2 L / ≈2 qt).
3. Brine 2.5%: dissolve 25 g (0.9 oz) salt in 1,000 mL (34 fl oz) water.
4. Bottom aromatics: garlic, oregano, pepper (and bay).
5. Pack strips tightly to reduce floating.
6. Add brine; keep 2–3 cm (¾–1 in) headspace.
7. De-bubble; place weight (use a cap if needed).
8. Ferment5–7 days at 64–68 °F (18–20 °C); burp if no airlock.
9. Taste from day 5; slight cloudiness is normal.
10. Refrigerate when ready; best within 4–5 weeks.

RECOMMENDED METHOD

- **Standard (cool room):** 5–7 days at 64–68 °F (18–20 °C) for vivid color and full flavor.
- **Hybrid (hot weather):** 12–24 h room temp, then fridge 1–2 weeks → crisper, cleaner profile.
- **Cold-ferment:** 2–3 weeks in fridge for gentle acidity and very firm texture.

2) HOT CHERRY PEPPERS

Ingredients

- **Hot cherry peppers, whole or halved:** 1,000 g (2.2 lb)
- **Garlic:** 4 cloves
- **Mustard seeds:** 1tsp
- **Black peppercorns:** 1 tsp
- **(Optional) Bay leaf:** 1
- **Brine:** 1,000 mL (34 fl oz) water+ 30 g (1.0 oz) salt (3%) — supports firmness of whole fruits

Step-by-Step

1. Wash and prick each pepper 2–3 times with a toothpick or halve and remove some seeds to moderate heat.
2. Jar: clean 2 L (≈2 qt).
3. Brine 3%: dissolve 30 g (1.0 oz) salt in 1,000 mL (34 fl oz) water.
4. Bottom: garlic, mustard, peppercorns (and bay).
5. Pack peppers snugly but don't crush.
6. Add brine; 2–3 cm (¾–1 in) headspace.
7. De-bubble; use a hefty weight (whole peppers float).
8. Ferment7–10 days at 64–68 °F (18–20 °C).
9. Taste from day 7; balanced heat and tang.
10. Refrigerate; best within 5–6 weeks.

Recommended Method

- **Standard (cool room):** 7–10 days at 64–68 °F (18–20 °C) to let brine penetrate whole fruits while keeping them firm.
- **Hybrid (hot weather):** 12–24 h room temp, then fridge 2–3 weeks → very crisp, clean heat.
- **Cold-ferment:** 3–4 weeks in fridge for a gentler profile and compact texture.

3) PEPPER-ONION MIX

Ingredients

- **Mixed sweet bell peppers, strips:** 700g (1.54 lb)
- **Red or white onion, thin rings:** 300 g (0.66 lb)
- **Dried oregano:** 1 tsp
- **Garlic:** 2 cloves
- **Red chili flakes:** ½–1 tsp (optional)
- **Brine:** 1,000 mL (34 fl oz) water + 25 g (0.9 oz) salt (2.5%)

Step-by-Step

1.Prep peppers(seed & membrane out; even strips) and slice onion into thin rings.
2.Jar: clean 2 L (≈2 qt). 3.Brine 2.5% as above.
4.Bottom: oregano, garlic (and chili if using).
5.Pack alternating layers of peppers and onion

to distribute density/aromatics.
6.Add brine; 2–3 cm (¾–1 in) headspace.
7.De-bubble; add weight (onion tends to float).
8.Ferment5–7 days at 64–68 °F (18–20 °C).
9.Taste from day 5; vegetal-sweet aroma is normal.
10.Refrigerate; best within 4–5 weeks (great on sandwiches, tacos, bowls).

Recommended Method

- **Standard (cool room):** 5–7 days at 64–68 °F (18–20 °C) to keep crunch and bright colors.
- **Hybrid (hot weather):** 12–24 h room temp, then fridge 1–2 weeks → cleaner profile, firmer bite.
- **Cold-ferment:** 2–3 weeks in fridge for gentle acidity and maximum crispness.

4.2 RECIPE SECTION (32)

4.2.7 ONIONS/SHALLOTS/GARLIC (4 RECIPES)

Basic equipment: 2 L (≈2 qt) jar for ~1,000 g (2.2 lb) batches; fermentation weights; long spoon; digital scale; optional airlock lid.
Headspace: 2–3 cm (¾–1 in).
Aroma note: a sulfurous smell in the first days is normal. For color and crunch, aim for 64–68 °F (18–20 °C).

1) RED ONION PETALS

Ingredients

- **Red onions, petals (separated wedges):** 1,000 g (2.2 lb)
- **Dried oregano:** 1 tsp
- **Black peppercorns:** 1 tsp
- **Bay leaf:** 1 (optional)
- **Brine:** 1,000 mL (34 fl oz) water + 25 g (0.9 oz) salt (2.5%)

Step-by-Step

1. Prep onions: trim ends, peel, separate into petals along natural lines.
2. Jar: clean and dry (2 L / ≈2 qt).
3. Brine 2.5%: dissolve 25 g (0.9 oz) salt in 1,000 mL (34 fl oz) water.
4. Bottom: oregano, pepper (and bay).
5. Pack petals snugly without crushing.
6. Cover with brine; keep 2–3 cm (¾–1 in) headspace.
7. De-bubble; add weight to submerge.
8. Ferment3–5 days at 64–68 °F (18–20 °C).
9. Taste from day 3; pinkish brine is normal.
10. Refrigerate; best within 3–4 weeks.

Recommended Method

- **Standard (cool room): 3**–5 days at 64–68 °F (18–20 °C) → bright color, lively crunch.
- **Hybrid (hot weather):** 12–24 h room temp, then fridge 1–2 weeks → cleaner profile, solid texture.
- **Cold-ferment:** 2–3 weeks in fridge for gentle acidity and firm bite.

2) FERMENTED SHALLOTS

Ingredients

- **Shallots, rounds 0.5–1 cm (¼–⅜ in) or small whole:** 1,000 g (2.2 lb)
- **Pink or black peppercorns:** 1 tsp
- **Dried thyme:** 1 tsp
- **Brine:**
  - ✓ **Rounds:** 1,000 mL (34 fl oz) water + 25 g (0.9 oz) salt (2.5%)
  - ✓ **Whole:** 1,000 mL (34 fl oz) water + 30 g (1.0 oz) salt (3%)

Step-by-Step

1. Peel shallots; slice into even rounds or keep small ones whole (score the top).
2. Jar: clean 2 L (≈2 qt).
3. Brine to match cut (2.5% rounds / 3% whole).
4. Bottom: pepper + thyme.
5. Pack shallots; don't over-compress.
6. Add brine; 2–3 cm (¾–1 in) headspace.
7. De-bubble; add weight.
8. Ferment5–7 days at 64–68 °F (18–20 °C) for rounds; 7–10 days for whole.
9. Taste for clean tang and shallot sweetness.
10. Refrigerate; best within 4–6 weeks.

Recommended Method

- **Standard (cool room):** 5–7 days (rounds) / 7–10 days (whole) at 64–68 °F (18–20 °C).
- **Hybrid (hot weather):** 12–24 h room temp, then fridge 1–2 weeks → better color and crunch.
- **Cold-ferment:** 2–3 weeks in fridge for sweeter notes and compact texture.

3) SPRING GARLIC SHOOTS

Ingredients

- **Garlic shoots (scapes), 1¼–2 in (3–5 cm) pieces:** 1,000 g (2.2 lb)
- **Lemon zest strips:** from 1 lemon
- **Black peppercorns:** 1tsp
- **Red chili flakes:** ½–1 tsp (optional)
- **Brine:** 1,000 mL (34 fl oz) water + 30 g (1.0 oz) salt (3%)

Step-by-Step

1. Wash & trim shoots (remove fibrous tips), cut pieces.
2. Jar: clean 2 L (≈2 qt).
3. Brine 3% as above.
4. Bottom: lemon zest, pepper (and chili).
5. Pack shoots evenly.
6. Add brine; 2–3 cm (¾–1 in) headspace.
7. De-bubble; add weight.
8. Ferment6–8 days at 64–68 °F (18–20 °C).
9. Taste from day 6; green/citrus notes shine.
10. Refrigerate; ideal within 4–5 weeks.

Recommended Method

- **Standard (cool room):** 6–8 days at 64–68 °F (18–20 °C) → superior crunch, vivid green flavor.
- **Hybrid (hot weather):** 12–24 h room temp, then fridge 1–2 weeks → cleaner profile, brighter color.
- **Cold-ferment:** 2–3 weeks in fridge for delicate taste and very firm texture.

4) THREE-CLOVE GARLIC

Ingredients

- **Garlic cloves, peeled, whole:** 1,000 g (2.2 lb)
- **Whole cloves (spice):** 3
- **Bay leaf:** 1
- **Black peppercorns:** 1tsp
- **(Optional) Orange zest:** strips from ½ orange
- **Brine:** 1,000 mL (34 fl oz) water +30g(1.0oz) salt (3%)

Step-by-Step

1. Peel cloves; if very large, lightly score one side.
2. Jar: clean 2 L (≈2 qt).
3. Brine 3% as above.
4. Bottom: cloves (spice), bay, pepper (and zest).
5. Pack garlic without crushing.
6. Add brine; 2–3 cm (¾–1 in) headspace.
7. De-bubble; use a hefty weight (cloves tend to float).
8. Ferment10–14 days at 64–68 °F (18–20 °C).
9. Taste from day 10; note: blue/green tint can appear—normal sulfur reaction.
10. Refrigerate; best within 6–8 weeks. Mince into dressings or use whole with meats/veg.

Recommended Method

- **Standard (cool room):** 10–14 days at 64–68 °F (18–20 °C) for even brine penetration and warm clove aroma.
- **Hybrid (hot weather):** 12–24 h room temp, then fridge 2–3 weeks → very firm cloves, gentler flavor.
- **Cold-ferment:** 3–4 weeks in fridge for delicate profile and maximal compactness.

The name plays on the double meaning: garlic + three whole cloves (the spice) for a warm, balsamic aroma.

4.2 RECIPE SECTION (32)

4.2.8CELERY / FENNEL / BEET/ CHARD (4 RECIPES)

Basicequipment:2 L (≈2qt) jarfor ~1,000 g(2.2 lb) batches; fermentation weights; long spoon; digital scale; optional airlock lid.

Headspace: 2–3 cm (¾–1 in).

Helpful notes: keep uniform cuts. For crispness, aim for 64–68 °F (18–20 °C). Fennel brine may go slightly cloudy (normal). Beet brine will turn red (normal).

1) CELERY STICKS

Ingredients

- **Celery stalks, de-stringed, sticks 3–4 in (8–10 cm):** 1,000 g (2.2 lb)
- **Garlic:** 2 cloves
- **Black peppercorns:** 1tsp
- **(Optional) Celery seeds:** 1 tsp • Bay leaf: 1
- **Brine:** 1,000 mL (34 fl oz) water + 30 g (1.0 oz) salt (3%)

Step-by-Step

1. Remove strings from outer ribs; cut even sticks.
2. Jar: clean 2 L (≈2 qt).
3. Brine 3%: dissolve 30 g (1.0 oz) salt in 1,000 mL (34 fl oz) water.
4. Bottom: garlic, pepper (celery seed/bay optional).
5. Pack upright, tight.
6. Add brine; 2–3 cm (¾–1 in) headspace.
7. De-bubble; add weight to submerge.
8. Ferment5–7 days at 64–68 °F (18–20 °C).
9. Taste from day 5.
10. Refrigerate; best within 4–5 weeks.

Recommended Method

- **Standard (cool room):** 5–7 days at 64–68 °F (18–20 °C) for top crunch.
- **Hybrid (hot weather):** 12–24 h room temp, then fridge 1–2 weeks → firmer texture.
- **Cold-ferment:** 2–3 weeks in fridge for gentle flavor and great crunch.

2) FENNEL & ORANGE

Ingredients

- **Fennel bulbs, wedges ½–¾ in (1–2 cm):** 1,000 g (2.2 lb)
- **Orange zest strips (no pith):** from 1 orange
- **Pink peppercorns or fennel seeds:** 1 tsp
- **Brine:** 1,000 mL (34 fl oz) water + 25 g (0.9 oz) salt (2.5%)

Step-by-Step

1. Trim bulbs; cut into even wedges (keep a bit of core attached).
2. Jar: clean 2 L (≈2 qt).
3. Brine 2.5%: dissolve 25 g (0.9 oz) salt in 1,000 mL (34 fl oz) water.
4. Bottom: half the zest + pink pepper/fennel seed.
5. Pack fennel; top with remaining zest.
6. Add brine; 2–3 cm (¾–1 in) headspace.
7. De-bubble; add weight.
8. Ferment5–7 days at 64–68 °F (18–20 °C).
9. Taste from day 5; bright anise–citrus.
10. Refrigerate; best within 4–5 weeks.

- **Standard (cool room)**: 5–7 days at 64–68 °F (18–20 °C) for fragrant profile and bright color.
- **Hybrid (hot weather):** 12–24 h room temp, then fridge 1–2 weeks → cleaner aromatics, excellent crunch.
- **Cold-ferment:** 2–3 weeks in fridge for very gentle notes.

3) BEET CUBES WITH CUMIN

Ingredients

- **Beetspeeled, ⅜–⅝ in (1–1.5 cm) cubes:** 1,000 g (2.2 lb)
- **Cumin seeds:** 1–2 tsp

  (Optional) Garlic: 1–2 cloves
- **Brine:** 1,000 mL (34 fl oz) water + 25 g (0.9 oz) salt (2.5%)

Step-by-Step

1.Peel and cut beets into even cubes. 2.Jar: clean 2 L (≈2 qt). 3.Brine 2.5% as above. 4.Bottom: cumin (and garlic if using). 5.Pack cubes gently. 6.Add brine; 2–3 cm (¾–1 in) headspace. 7.De-bubble; add weight. 8.Ferment7–10 days at 64–68 °F (18–20 °C). 9.Taste from day 7; red brine and slight fizz are normal.

10.Refrigerate;bestwithin5–6 weeks.

Recommended Method

- **Standard(coolroom):** 7–10 days at 64–68 °F (18–20 °C) for rounded cumin and balanced tang.
- **Hybrid (hot weather):** 12–24 h room temp, then fridge 1–2 weeks → brighter color, compact texture.
- **Cold-ferment:** 2–3+ weeks in fridge for gentle profile.

4) RAINBOW CHARD STEMS

Ingredients

- **Chard stems peeled (remove fibrous edges), 1¼–2 in (3–5 cm) batons:** 1,000 g (2.2 lb)
- **Lemon zest strips:** from 1 lemon
- **Garlic:** 1 clove
- (Optional) **Red chili flakes:** ½ tsp
- **Brine:** 1,000 mL (34 fl oz) water + 30 g (1.0 oz) salt (3%)

Step-by-Step

1. Peel outer fibers; cut even batons.
2. Jar: clean 2 L (≈2 qt).
3. Brine 3% as above.
4. Bottom: lemon zest, garlic (and chili).
5. Pack without over-compressing.
6. Add brine; 2–3 cm (¾–1 in) headspace.
7. De-bubble; add weight.
8. Ferment4–6 days at 64–68 °F (18–20 °C).
9. Taste from day 4; expect bright citrus and vivid color.
10. Refrigerate; best within 3–4 weeks.

Recommended Method

- **Standard (cool room):** 4–6 days at 64–68 °F (18–20 °C) for firm, crunchy stems.
- **Hybrid (hot weather):** 12–24 h room temp, then fridge 1–2 weeks → extra crunch.
- **Cold-ferment:** 2–3 weeks in fridge for delicate flavor and compact bite.

CHAPTER 5

DRY-SALT FERMENTS: KRAUT & MIXES (20 RECIPES)

5.1 METHODS & STEP-BY-STEP PROCEDURES

5.1.1FINESLICING•SALTING& MASSAGING•PACKING/PRESSING•SELF-BRINING • TEMPERATURE

Basicgear

- Sharp knife or mandoline; large bowl (4–5 qt / 4–5 L); scale; tamper/wooden spoon; wide-mouth jars; weights and optional airlock lid.

Jar sizing (quick guide)

- 800–1,000 g (1.8–2.2 lb) shredded veg →1 L (≈1 qt)
- 1,500 g (3.3 lb) → 1.5 L (≈1.5 qt)
- 2,000 g (4.4 lb) → 2 L (≈2 qt)
- Always leave 2–3 cm (¾–1 in) headspace.

Step 1 — Fine, even slicing

- Remove damaged outer leaves and the tough core as needed.
- Slice to 1–2 mm (≈1/16–1/12 in) for classic kraut; up to 3 mm (≈1/8 in) for rustic mixes.
- Uniform cuts = even ferment and faster self-brining.

Step 2 — Weigh & calculate salt

- Weigh cleaned vegetables.
- Use 2% salt by vegetable weight (handy range 1.8–2.2%; go 2.5% in warm rooms or for extra crunch).
- Formula: salt (g) = veg weight (g) × 0.02.
  - ✓ Example A: 1,200 g (2.65 lb) →24 g (0.85 oz) salt.
  - ✓ Example B: 800 g (1.76 lb) →16 g (0.56 oz) salt.
  - ✓ Example C: 5 lb (≈2,270 g) →45 g (1.6 oz) salt.

Tip: a scale is best. If you must estimate: 1 level tsp kosher salt ≈ 5–6 g (0.18–0.21 oz) (approximate, brand-dependent).

Step 3 — Salt & massage (draw out brine)

1. Put sliced veg in the bowl; sprinkle all the salt evenly.
2. Toss & squeeze 1–2 min.
3. Rest 15–30 min (covered) for osmosis to start the self-brine.
4. Massage another 2–5 min until you see puddles of liquid and the shreds feel pliable.
   - ✓ If brine is still low after 30–40 min total, see “Top-up” below.

Step 4 — Pack/press into the jar

1. Add ahandfultothejarandpress firmly with a tamper/spoon until brine rises above that layer.
2. Repeat in layers until full.
3. Target 1–2 cm (⅜–¾ in) of brine above the packed veg.
4. Add a cabbage leaf or food-grade disc and a weight to keep everything below brine.

Step 5 — Lid, burping & daily care

- Closewithan airlock oruse aplain lid and burp once daily for the first 3–5 days.
- In early days, press down if veg try to float.
- Rule#1: keep itsubmerged at all times.

Step 6 — Self-brine: if you're short

- After massaging, if brine doesn't cover by 1–2 cm, either massage 1–2 min more or top up with a 2% brine: 20 g (0.7 oz) salt in 1,000 mL (34 fl oz) water—add just
- enough to cover.

Step 7 — Temperature, timeline & tasting

- Sweet spot: 64–68 °F (18–20 °C) for clean flavor and crunch.
  - ✓ Warmer (70–75 °F / 21–24 °C): faster (5–10 days) but softer texture.
  - ✓ Cooler (59–63 °F / 15–17 °C): slower, finer flavor (2–4 weeks).
- Typical plan: taste on day 3–5–7, then week 2; refrigerate when acidity tastes right to you.

Quick cues (normal vs not)

- Normal: bubbles, slight haze, fresh sour aroma.
- Not normal: colored molds, rotten smell, slimy texture → discard.

5.2.1 SAUERKRAUT (6 RECIPES)

Basic gear: 4–5 qt (4–5 L) bowl, mandoline/knife, scale, 1 L (≈1 qt) jar for ~1,000 g (2.2 lb) sliced veg, weight and optional airlock.

Salt guide: 2% of vegetable weight (e.g., 1,000 g → 20 g (0.7 oz) salt).

Headspace: 2–3 cm (¾–1 in). Temperature: 64–68 °F (18–20 °C).

1) CLASSIC WHITE

Ingredients (1 L/≈1 qt)

- Green/white cabbage, finely sliced: 1,000 g (2.2 lb)
- Salt: 20 g (0.7 oz) (2% of veg weight)

Step-by-Step

1. Slice to 1–2 mm (≈1/16–1/12 in); remove tough core.
2. Weigh & salt: add 20 g (0.7 oz) salt.
3. Massage 1–2 min → rest 15–30 min → massage 2–5 min until ample self-brine forms.
4. Taste a shred for pleasant saltiness.
5. Pack & press in layers until 1–2 cm (⅜–¾ in) brine sits above the veg.
6. Cap with a leaf/disc; place weight to keep submerged.
7. Close (airlock or plain lid) and burp daily for 3–5 days.
8. Ferment at 64–68 °F (18–20 °C).
9. Taste on day 3–5–7, then week 2.
10. Refrigerate when right; keeps 4–8 weeks.

Recommended Method

Standard: 10–14 days at 64–68 °F (18–20 °C) for clean profile and crunch.

Warm rooms: use 2.25–2.5% salt or chill earlier.

Cold-ferment: fridge-only 3–4 weeks (gentle tang, max crunch).

2) RED CABBAGE & APPLE

Ingredients (1 L/≈1 qt)

- Red cabbage,finelysliced: 800 g (1.76 lb)
  Crisp apple, fine julienne: 200 g (0.44 lb)
- Salt: 20 g (0.7 oz) (2% of total 1,000 g)

Step-by-Step

1. Slice cabbage; julienne apple.
2. Weigh total (cabbage+apple = 1,000 g) and add 20 g salt.
3. Massage & rest until strong self-brine appears.
4. Pack & press; ensure 1–2 cm brine above.
5. Leaf/disc + weight to submerge.
6. Close & burp daily at first.
7. Ferment at 64–68 °F (18–20 °C); apple sugars speed up.
8. Taste on day 3–5.
9. Top up if needed with 2% brine (20 g salt in 1,000 mL / 34 fl oz water).
10. Refrigerate; best 3–6 weeks.

Recommended Method

- **Standard:** 7–10 daysat 64–68 °F (18–20 °C) (bright fruit, vivid color).
- **Warm rooms:** 2.25–2.5% salt or chill when ready.
- **Cold-ferment:** 3–4 weeks in fridge for softer fruit notes.

3) BAVARIAN CARAWAY

Ingredients (1 L/≈1 qt)

- **Green/white cabbage, sliced:** 1,000 g (2.2 lb)
- **Salt:** 20 g (0.7 oz) (2%)
- **Caraway seeds:** 1–2tsp(≈2–4 g / 0.07–0.14 oz)

Step-by-Step

1. Slice fine; salt with 20 g.
2. Add caraway, massage & rest until pliable and briny.
3. Pack & press; 1–2 cm brine above.
4. Leaf/disc + weight; close & burp.
5. Ferment at 64–68 °F (18–20 °C).
6. Taste day 5–7, then week 2.
7. Refrigerate when right; keeps 4–8 weeks.

Recommended Method

- **Standard**: 10–14 days at 64–68 °F (18–20 °C) for integrated spice and crunch.
- **Warm rooms:** 2.25% salt or chill early.
- **Cold-ferment:** 3–4 weeks in fridge for gentler spice.

4) GARLIC & JUNIPER

Ingredients (1 L/≈1 qt)

- **Green/white cabbage, sliced:** 1,000 g (2.2 lb)
- **Salt:** 20 g (0.7 oz) (2%)
  Garlic, finely minced: 2–3 cloves
- **Juniper berries, lightly crushed:** 6–8 (≈ 1 tsp)

Step-by-Step

1. Combine cabbage, salt, garlic, juniper.
2. Massage & rest to build self-brine.
3. Pack & press; keep 1–2 cm brine above.
4. Leaf/disc + weight; close & burp.
5. Ferment at 64–68 °F (18–20 °C).
6. Tasteday 5–7; garlic mellows by day 10–14.
7. Top up with 2% brine if short.
8. Refrigerate; keeps 4–8 weeks.

Recommended Method

- **Standard:**10–14days at 64–68 °F (18–20 °C) (balsamic juniper, rounded garlic).
- **Warm rooms:** 2.25–2.5% salt or chill earlier.
- **Cold-ferment:** 3–4 weeks fridge for softer edges.

5) GOLDEN TURMERIC

- **Green/white cabbage, sliced:** 1,000 g (2.2 lb)
- **Salt:** 20 g (0.7 oz) (2%)
  Fresh turmeric matchsticks 10–15 g (0.35–0.53 oz) or turmeric powder 1–2 tsp
  Black pepper, ground: ½ tsp

Step-by-Step

1. Mix cabbage, salt, turmeric, pepper.
2. Massage & rest until a golden brine forms.
3. Pack & press; 1–2 cm brine above.
4. Leaf/disc + weight; close & burp.
5. Ferment at 64–68 °F (18–20 °C).
6. Tasteday 5–7; nicely integrated by day 7–12.
7. Refrigerate; keeps 4–8 weeks.

Recommended Method

- **Standard:** 7–12 daysat64–68 °F (18–20 °C) (bright spice, vivid color).
- **Warm rooms:** 2.25% salt or chill when ready.
- **Cold-ferment:** 3–4 weeks in fridge for milder notes.

6) SMOKY PAPRIKA

Ingredients (1 L/≈1 qt)

Green/whitecabbage, sliced: 1,000 g (2.2 lb)
Salt: 20 g (0.7 oz) (2%)

- **Smoked paprika (pimentón):** 1–2 tsp
- **(Optional) Garlic, minced:** 1 clove

Step-by-Step

1. Combine cabbagewith salt,paprika (and garlic).
2. Massage & rest until self-brine builds.
3. Pack & press; ensure 1–2 cm brine above.
4. Leaf/disc + weight; close & burp.
5. Ferment at 64–68 °F (18–20 °C).
6. Tasteday 5–7; smoke mellows by day 7–12.
7. Refrigerate; keeps4–8 weeks.

Recommended Method

- **Standard:** 7–12daysat 64–68 °F (18–20 °C) (soft smoke, clean tang).
- **Warm rooms:** 2.25% salt or early chill.
- **Cold-ferment:** 3–4 weeks fridge for gentle smoke.

5.2.2 FERMENTED SLAWS (4 RECIPES)

Basic gear: 4–5 qt (4–5 L)bowl,mandoline/knife,scale,1L(≈1qt)jarfor~1,000 g (2.2 lb) sliced veg, weight and optional airlock.

Saltguide:2%oftotal veg weight(e.g.,1,000 g → 20g (0.7oz) salt).

Headspace:2–3 cm(¾–1in).Temperature:64–68 °F(18–20°C).

Top-up(if needed):add 2%brine (20 g / 0.7 ozsaltin1,000 mL/ 34flozwater)justtocover.

1)CABBAGE–CARROT SLAW

Ingredients(1L / ≈1qt)

- **Green/whitecabbage,finely sliced:** 800 g (1.76 lb)
- **Carrot, fine julienne or coarse-grated:** 200 g (0.44 lb)
- **Salt:** 20g(0.7oz)(2%total)
- **(Optional) Caraway seeds:** 1tsp(≈2g/ 0.07 oz)

Step-by-Step

1.Slice cabbage 1–2 mm; cut carrot fine julienne.

2.Weigh total = 1,000 g (2.2 lb); add 20 g (0.7 oz) salt (+ caraway, optional).

3.Massage 1–2 min → rest 15–30 min → massage 2–5 min until self-brine forms.

4.Pack & press in layers until brine sits 1–2 cm (⅜–¾ in) above the veg.

5.Leaf/disc + weight to keep submerged.

6.Close (airlock or lid) and burp daily for 3–5 days.

7.Ferment at 64–68 °F (18–20 °C); taste day 5–7.

8.Refrigerate when ready; keeps 4–8 weeks.

Recommended Method

- **Standard:** 7–10 days at 64–68 °F (18–20 °C) (crisp, clean).
- **Warm rooms:** 2.25% salt or chill right at target.
- **Cold-ferment:** fridge-only 3–4 weeks (gentler, extra crunch).

2) CABBAGE–BEET SLAW

Ingredients (1 L / ≈1 qt)

- **Green/white cabbage, finelysliced:** 700g (1.54 lb)
- **Beet, peeled, fine julienne:** 300 g (0.66 lb)
  Salt: 20 g (0.7 oz) (2% total)
- (**Optional) Cumin seeds:** 1tsp

Step-by-Step

1. Slice cabbage; julienne beet.
2. Weigh 1,000 g (2.2 lb) total; add 20 g (0.7 oz) salt (+ cumin optional).
3. Massage & rest until a red self-brine develops.
4. Pack & press; ensure 1–2 cm brine above.
5. Leaf/disc + weight; close & burp.
6. Ferment at 64–68 °F (18–20 °C); taste day 6–8.
7. Refrigerate; best within 5–6 weeks (red brine is normal).

Recommended Method

- **Standard:** 8–12 days at 64–68 °F (18–20 °C) (vivid color, rounded tang).
- **Warm rooms:** 2.25% salt or chill earlier.
- **Cold-ferment:** 3–4 weeks in fridge for softer earthy notes.

3)NAPA SLAW

Ingredients(1L / ≈1qt)

- **Napa cabbage, cross-cut strips ½–¾ in (1–2 cm):** 900 g (1.98 lb)
- **Scallions, thin rings:** 100 g (0.22 lb)
- **Salt:** 20 g (0.7 oz) (2% total)
- **(Optional) Fresh ginger, matchsticks:** 10 g (0.35 oz)

Step-by-Step

1. Cross-cut Napa; slice scallions thin.
2. Weigh total; add 20 g salt (+ ginger optional).
3. Massage briefly (Napa releases lots of water) →rest 15 min →massage until pliable.
4. Pack & press; keep 1–2 cm (⅜–¾ in) brine above.
5. Leaf/disc + weight; close & burp.
6. Ferment at 64–68 °F (18–20 °C); taste day 3–5 (shorter timeline).
7. Refrigerate; enjoy within 3–5 weeks.

Recommended Method

- **Standard:** 4–6 days at 64–68 °F (18–20 °C) (fresh, crisp).
- **Warm rooms:** 2.25–2.5% salt to hold firmness or chill earlier.
- **Cold-ferment:** 2–3 weeks in fridge (very gentle).

4) APPLE–FENNEL SLAW

Ingredients(1L / ≈1qt)

- **Fennel, thinly shaved (mandoline):** 700 g (1.54 lb)

  Crisp apple, fine julienne: 250 g (0.55 lb)
- **Lemon zest strips (no pith):** from ½ lemon (optional)
- **Fennel seeds or pink peppercorns:** 1 1 tsp
- **Salt**: 20 g (0.7 oz) (2% total)

Recommended Method

- **Standard:** 5–7 days at 64–68 °F (18–20 °C) (anise–citrus–apple in balance).
- **Warm rooms:** 2.25–2.5% salt or chill at target (fruit speeds ferment).
- **Cold-ferment:** 2–3 weeks in fridge for gentler profile.

Step-by-Step

1. Shavefennel; julienne apple; add zest and fennel seeds/pink pepper.
2. Weigh 1,000 g (2.2 lb) total; add 20 g salt.
3. Massage & rest until self-brine forms (apple sugars speed things up).
4. Pack & press; maintain 1–2 cm brine above.
5. Leaf/disc + weight; close & burp.
6. Ferment at 64–68 °F (18–20 °C); taste day 4–6.
7. Refrigerate; best within 3–5 weeks.

5.2.3 CURTIDO (3 RECIPES)

Basic gear: 4–5 qt (4–5 L) bowl,mandoline/knife,scale,1L(≈1qt)jar for ~1,000 g (2.2 lb) sliced veg, weight and optional airlock.

Saltguide:2%oftotal weight(e.g.,1,000 g → 20g / 0.7 oz).

Headspace: 2–3 cm (¾–1 in). Temperature: 64–68 °F (18–20 °C).

Top-up(if needed):cover with2%brine (20 g / 0.7 ozsaltin 1,000 mL/ 34flozwater), just enough to submerge.

1)MILD SALVADORAN CURTIDO

Step-by-Step

1. Slice cabbage(1–2 mm), julienne carrot, thin-slice onion.
2. Weigh total (1,000 g / 2.2 lb) and add salt + oregano (and jalapeño if using).
3. Massage 1–2 min → rest 15–30 min → massage 2–5 min until self-brine forms.
4. Pack & press into the jar in layers until brine sits 1–2 cm (⅜–¾ in)above the veg.
5. Leaf/disc + weight to keep submerged.
6. Close (airlock or lid) and burp daily for 3–5 days.
7. Ferment at 64–68 °F (18–20 °C); taste day 4–6.
8. Refrigerate when right; keeps 3–6 weeks.

Ingredients (1 L / ≈1 qt)

- **Green/white cabbage, finely sliced:** 750 g (1.65 lb)
- **Carrot, fine julienne:** 150 g (0.33 lb)
- **Red onion, very thin slices:** 100g(0.22 lb)
- **Dried oregano (Mexican preferred):** 1–2 tsp (≈ 1–2 g / 0.04–0.07 oz)
- **(Optional) Mild jalapeño or green pepper, thin rings:** 0–½ small (0–15 g / 0–0.5 oz)
- **Salt:** 20 g (0.7 oz) (2% of total 1,000 g)

Recommended Method

- **Standard:**4–7 daysat 64–68 °F (18–20 °C) (crisp, delicate, herbal).
- **Warm rooms:** raise salt to 2.25–2.5% or chill when ready.
- **Cold-ferment:** fridge-only 2–3 weeks for a very gentle profile.

2) SPICY CURTIDO

Ingredients (1 L / ≈1 qt)

- Green/white cabbage, finely sliced: 750 g (1.65 lb)
- Carrot, fine julienne: 150 g (0.33 lb)
- Red onion, thin slices: 80 g (0.18 lb)
- Jalapeño or serrano, thin rings: 1–2 small (20–30 g / 0.7–1.1 oz)
- Dried oregano (Mexican preferred): 1–2 tsp (≈ 1–2 g / 0.04–0.07 oz)
- (Optional) Red chili flakes: ½–1 tsp; minced garlic 1 clove
- Salt: 20 g (0.7 oz) (2% of 1,000 g total)

Step-by-Step

1. Slice cabbage, carrot, onion; cut chiles into thin rings.
2. Weigh and add salt + oregano (and flakes/garlic if using).
3. Massage & rest until a generous self-brine forms.
4. Pack & press; ensure 1–2 cm brine above.
5. Leaf/disc + weight; close & burp.
6. Ferment at 64–68 °F (18–20 °C); taste day 5–8 (heat builds over time).
7. Refrigerate; best within 3–6 weeks.

Recommended Method

- **Standard:** 5–8 days at 64–68 °F (18–20 °C) (integrated spice, clear heat).
- **Warm rooms:** 2.25–2.5% salt or chill earlier.
- **Cold-ferment:** 2–3+ weeks in fridge for softer heat and excellent crunch.

3) PINEAPPLE CURTIDO

Ingredients(1L / ≈1qt)

- **Green/white cabbage, finely sliced:** 700 g (1.54 lb)
- **Pineapple, small dice ¼ in (½ cm):** 200 g (0.44 lb)
- **Red onion, thin slices:** 100 g (0.22 lb)
- **Dried oregano (Mexican preferred):** 1 tsp (≈ 1 g / 0.04 oz)
- **(Optional) Mild fresh chile:** 0–½ small (0–15 g / 0–0.5 oz)
- **Salt:** 20 g (0.7 oz) (2% of 1,000 g total)

Step-by-Step

1. Slice cabbage & onion; dice pineapple small.
2. Weigh total; add salt + oregano (chile optional).
3. Massage 1–2 min → rest 10–20 min (fruit sugars speed brine) →massage 1–3 min until ample brine.
4. Pack & press; keep 1–2 cm brine above.
5. Leaf/disc + weight; close & burp.
6. Ferment at 64–68 °F (18–20 °C); taste day 3–5 (faster ferment).
7. Refrigerate when right; best within 3–5 weeks.

Recommended Method

- **Standard:** 3–5daysat64–68 °F (18–20 °C) (bright fruit, lively tang).
- **Warm rooms:** consider 2.25% salt or a hybrid approach (12–24 h room temp, then fridge 1–2 weeks).
- **Cold-ferment:** 2–3 weeks in fridge for softer tropical notes.

5.2.4 CRUNCHY MIXES (4 RECIPES)

Basic gear: 4–5 qt (4–5 L) bowl, mandoline/knife, scale, 1 L (≈1 qt) jar for ~1,000 g (2.2 lb) sliced veg, weight and optional airlock.

Salt guide: 2% of total veg weight (e.g., 1,000 g → 20 g / 0.7 oz salt).

Headspace: 2–3 cm (¾–1 in). Temperature: 64–68 °F (18–20 °C).

Top-up (if needed): add 2% brine (20 g / 0.7 oz salt in 1,000 mL / 34 fl oz water) just to cover.

Crispness note: keep uniform cuts (1–2 mm for cabbage; matchsticks/julienne for the crunchy veg),

packfirmly, andkeepeverything belowbrine.

1) GARDEN CRUNCH

Ingredients(1L / ≈1qt)

Green/white cabbage, finely sliced: 600 g (1.32 lb) Carrot, fine julienne: 150 g (0.33 lb) Celery, matchsticks: 150 g (0.33 lb) Radish, thin rounds: 100 g (0.22 lb) Celery seed or mustard seed: 1 tsp (≈ 2 g / 0.07 oz) Black peppercorns, lightly crushed: ½–1 tsp Salt: 20 g (0.7 oz) (2% of 1,000 g total)

Recommended Method

- **Standard:** 7–10 days at 64–68 °F (18–20 °C) → high crunch, clean profile.
- **Warm rooms**: 2.25% salt or chill at target.
- **Cold-ferment:** fridge-only 3–4 weeks for max crunch.

Step-by-Step

1. Slice/julienne all veg; add seeds and pepper.
2. Weigh total (1,000 g) and add 20 g salt.
3. Massage 1–2 min → rest 15–30 min → massage 2–5 min until self-brine forms.
4. Pack & press into the jar until 1–2 cm (⅜–¾ in) brine sits above the veg.
5. Leaf/disc + weight to keep submerged; close and burp daily (3–5 days).
6. Ferment at 64–68 °F (18–20 °C); taste day 5–7.
7. Refrigerate when right; best within 4–6 weeks.

2) DILL-PICKLE KRAUT

Ingredients (1 L / ≈1 qt)

- **Green/white cabbage, finely sliced:** 900 g (1.98 lb)
- **Fresh dill, roughly chopped:** 10–15 g (0.35–0.53 oz)
- **Dill seedor mustard seed:** 1 tsp (≈ 2 g / 0.07 oz)
- **Garlic, finely minced:** 1–2 cloves
  (Optional) Firm cucumber, matchsticks: 100 g (0.22 lb)
- **Salt:** 20 g (0.7 oz) (2% of 1,000 g total)

Step-by-Step

1. Slice cabbage; chop dill; (optional) cut cucumber firm matchsticks.
2. Weigh and add salt + dill (fresh and/or seed) + garlic.
3. Massage & rest until a strong self-brine forms.
4. Pack & press; keep 1–2 cm brine above.
5. Leaf/disc + weight; close & burp.
6. Ferment at 64–68 °F (18–20 °C); taste day 5–7.
7. Refrigerate; keeps 4–6 weeks.

Recommended Method

- **Standard:** 3–5daysat 64–68 °F (18–20 °C) (bright fruit, lively tang).
- **Warm rooms:** consider 2.25% salt or a hybrid approach (12–24 h room temp, then fridge 1–2 weeks).
- **Cold-ferment:** 2–3 weeks in fridge for softer tropical notes.

3) GINGER–LIME KRAUT

Ingredients (1 L / ≈1 qt)

- **Green/white cabbage, finely sliced:** 950g(2.09 lb)
- **Fresh ginger, matchsticks:** 15–20 g (0.53–0.71 oz)
- **Lime zest (no pith):** from 1–2 limes
- **(Optional) Kaffir lime leaf:** 1 small, torn
- **(Optional, at serving):** 1–2 tsp (5–10 mL / 0.17–0.34 fl oz) lime juice
- **Salt:** 20 g (0.7 oz) (2% of 1,000 g total)

Step-by-Step

1. Slice cabbage; add ginger, zest (and kaffir leaf if using).
2. Weigh and add 20 g salt.
3. Massage & rest until a fragrant self-brine forms.
4. Pack & press; maintain 1–2 cm brine above.
5. Leaf/disc + weight; close & burp.
6. Ferment at 64–68 °F (18–20 °C); taste day 5–7.
7. Refrigerate; best within 4–6 weeks.

Tip:addatouchof lime juice only when serving, not during the ferment.

Recommended Method

- **Standard:** 7–10 days at 64–68 °F (18–20 °C) (bright citrus, lively ginger).
- **Warm rooms:** 2.25% salt or chill at target.
- **Cold-ferment:** 3–4 weeks fridge for softer citrus and max crunch.

4) HERB & LEMON ZEST

Ingredients(1L / ≈1qt)

- **Green/white cabbage, finely sliced:** 900 g (1.98 lb)
- **Mixed fresh herbs (parsley, dill, thyme, oregano), roughly chopped:** 10–12 g (0.35–0.42 oz)
- **Lemon zest (no pith):** from 1 lemon
- **Black pepper, ground:** ¼–½ tsp (optional)
- **Garlic, very finely minced:** 1 clove (optional)
- **Salt:** 20g(0.7 oz) (2% of 1,000 g total)

Step-by-Step

1. Slice cabbage 1–2 mm; addsalt, chili flakes(and garlicif using).
2. Massage 1–2 min → rest 15–30 min → massage 2–5 min until self-brine forms.
3. Pack & press; keep 1–2 cm (⅜–¾ in) brine above the veg.
4. Leaf/disc + weight; close and burp daily for 3–5 days.
5. Ferment at 64–68 °F (18–20 °C); taste day 5–7.
6. Refrigerate when right; keeps 4–8 weeks.

Recommended Method

- **Standard:** 7–10 days at 64–68 °F (18–20 °C) → clear heat, high crunch.
- **Warm rooms:**2.25% salt or chill at target.
- **Cold-ferment:**fridge-only 3–4 weeks for softer heat.

5.2.5 SPICY/CITRUS VARIANTS (3 RECIPES)

Basic gear: 4–5 qt (4–5 L) bowl,mandoline/knife,scale,1L(≈1qt)jarfor~1,000g(2.2 lb) sliced veg, weight and optional airlock.

Salt guide: 2% of total weight (e.g., 1,000 g → 20 g / 0.7 oz).

Headspace: 2–3 cm (¾–1 in). Temperature: 64–68 °F (18–20 °C).

Top-up (if needed): 2% brine (20 g / 0.7 oz salt in 1,000 mL / 34 fl oz water), just enough to cover.

Heat/citrus note: wear gloves for chiles. Use zest (no bitter pith). Add citrus juice only when serving, not during ferment.

1) CHILI-FLAKE KRAUT

Ingredients (1 L / ≈1 qt)

- **Green/white cabbage, finely sliced:** 1,000 g (2.2 lb)
- **Salt:** 20 g(0.7oz)(2%)
- **Red chili flakes (or gochugaru):** 1–3 tsp (to taste)
- **(Optional) Garlic, finely minced:** 1 clove

Step-by-Step

1. Slice/julienne all veg; add seeds and pepper.
2. Weigh total (1,000 g) and add 20 g salt.
3. Massage 1–2 min → rest 15–30 min → massage 2–5 min until self-brine forms.
4. Pack & press into the jar until 1–2 cm (⅜–¾ in) brine sits above the veg.
5. Leaf/disc + weight to keep submerged; close and burp daily (3–5 days).
6. Ferment at 64–68 °F (18–20 °C); taste day 5–7.
7. Refrigerate when right; best within 4–6 weeks.

Recommended Method

- **Standard:** 7–10 days at 64–68 °F (18–20 °C) → high crunch, clean profile.
- **Warm rooms:** 2.25% salt or chill at target.
- **Cold-ferment:** fridge-only 3–4 weeks for max crunch.

2) JALAPEÑO-LIME

Ingredients (1 L / ≈1 qt)

- **Green/whitecabbage, finely sliced:** 900g(1.98 lb)
- **Jalapeño, thin rings (seeded for less heat):** 100 g (0.22 lb)
- **Lime zest (no pith):** from 1–2 limes
- **(Optional)** Freshcilantro at serving
- **Salt:** 20g(0.7oz)(2% of 1,000 g total)

Step-by-Step

1. Slice cabbage & jalapeño; add lime zest.
2. Weigh total (1,000 g / 2.2 lb); add 20 g (0.7 oz) salt.
3. Massage & rest until a fragrant self-brine forms.
4. Pack & press; ensure 1–2 cm brine above.
5. Leaf/disc + weight; close & burp.
6. Ferment at 64–68 °F (18–20 °C); taste day 5–7.
7. Refrigerate; at serving, add a few drops of lime juice and cilantro.Keeps 4–6weeks.

Recommended Method

- **Standard:** 7–10 days at 64–68 °F (18–20 °C) (bright citrus, balanced heat).
- **Warm rooms:** 2.25% salt or chill when ready.
- **Cold-ferment:** 3–4 weeks in fridge for gentler lime and very firm texture.

3) ORANGE ZEST & BLACK PEPPER

Ingredients (1 L / ≈1 qt)

- **Green/whitecabbage,finely sliced:** 950 g (2.09 lb)
- **Orange zest (no pith), strips:** from 1–2 oranges
- **Black peppercorns, lightly crushed:** ½–1 tsp
- **(Optional) Bay leaf:** 1
- **Salt:** 20 g (0.7 oz) (2% of 1,000 g total)

Step-by-Step

1. Slice cabbage; add zest, pepper (and bay).
2. Salt with 20 g (0.7 oz); massage 1–2 min → rest 15–30 min → massage 2–5 min.
3. Pack & press; keep 1–2 cm brine above.
4. Leaf/disc + weight; close & burp.
5. Ferment at 64–68 °F (18–20 °C); taste day 5–7 (citrus integrates by day 7–12).
6. Refrigerate; best within 4–6 weeks.

Recommended Method

- **Standard:** 7–12 days at 64–68 °F (18–20 °C) (bright citrus, rounded pepper).
- **Warm rooms:** 2.25% salt or chill early.
- **Cold-ferment:** 3–4 weeks in fridge for softer citrus notes

CHAPTER 6

FERMENTED CONDIMENTS & SAUCES (16 RECIPES)

6.1 METHODS & STEP-BY-STEP PROCEDURES

6.1.1 PRIMARY FERMENT • BLENDING • MATURATION • BOTTLING • STORAGE

Basicgear

- Wide-mouth jars with weights/airlocks (0.5–2 L / 1–2 qt), large bowl, scale, knife/mandoline, blender/processor, funnel and woozy bottles, optional sieve/chinois, pH strips or meter (optional), gloves (for chiles).

A) Process choices: Mash (dry-salt) vs Brine

Mash method (dry-salt, self-brine)

- Great for chiles, garlic, herbs, onion/shallot, thick mixes.
- Salt: typically 2–3% of veg weight.
  - ✓ Example: 1,000 g (2.2 lb) chiles →20–30 g (0.7–1.0 oz) salt.
- Pros: concentrated flavor, thicker body. Cons: denser → pack/degas well.

Brine method (whole pieces under brine)

- Best for watery veg/fruit and pourable sauces.
- Common brine: 2.0–2.5% (e.g., 20–25 g / 0.7–0.9 oz salt per 1,000 mL / 34 fl oz water).
- Pros: easy to tune thickness later. Cons: slight dilution; may need straining.

Golden rule: no oil in the primary ferment. Add oils only after fermentation, at serving or finishing.

B) Primary ferment (7 steps)

1.Prep & weigh uniformly cut produce (seed/de-rib chiles if reducing heat).

2. Salt
   - ✓ Mash: mix salt into produce (2–3%).
   - ✓ Brine: make brine (2.0–2.5%) and fully cover.

3. Pack & submerge; add weight; leave 2–3 cm (¾–1 in) headspace.

4. Temperature & timeline
   - ✓ 64–68 °F (18–20 °C) sweet spot.
   - ✓ Typical windows: chiles/garlic 7–14 d (mash) • 5–10 d (brine). Fruit 3–6 d (use 2.5–3%
   - ✓ salt in warm rooms).

5. Daily care: with non-airlock lids burp daily for the first 3–5 days. Keep every bit below brine.

6. Normal vs not
   - ✓ Normal: bubbles, slight haze, bright sour/vegetal aroma.
   - ✓ Not: colored molds, rotten smell, sliminess → discard.

7. (Optional) pH check

- Lactic sauces commonly sit around ≈3.5–4.2. Lower = sharper. Refrigerate after processing regardless.

C) Blending & texture tuning

1. **Drain (for brine batches) and reserve brine.**
2. **Blend to desired smoothness.**
3. **Adjust:**

- Thinner→ add reserved brine by spoonfuls: 15–60 mL (1–4 Tbsp / 0.5–2 fl oz).
- Silky→ strain through fine sieve/chinois.
- Thicker→ fold back some solids.
- No oils yet; add only after fermentation.

4. Post-blend (optional)

- Vinegar (5%): 1–3 tsp (5–15 mL) per ~500 mL (17 fl oz) for rounding.
- Sweetener: 1–3% to soften heat (after ferment).
- Stabilizer (optional, after ferment): xanthan 0.1–0.2% (1–2 g per 1,000 g / 2.2 lb),
- blend thoroughly.
- Capsaicin caution: blending hot peppers aerosolizes heat—use lid, gloves, and ventilate.

D) Maturation (flavor conditioning)

- Move blended sauce to a jar with airlock or a lid left a touch loose:
  - Cool room (64–68 °F / 18–20 °C): 3–7 days to knit flavors.
  - Fridge: 1–3 weeks for slower, rounder integration.
- Degas if pressurized; stir or shake every 2–3 days.

E) Bottling

1. Clean bottles (warm if the sauce was heated).
2. Funnel + optional sieve for smooth fills.
3. Fill leaving 1–2 cm (⅜–¾ in) headspace.
4. Cap firmly; if still lively, don't overtighten and monitor.

Optional gentle pasteurization: brief heat to a light simmer before hot-filling extends life but removes most probiotics and can shift flavor.

F)Storage & use

- Refrigerate: typically 4–8 weeks for unpasteurized sauces (often longer if clean and acidic).
- Shake before use (natural separation).
- Discard if odd smells, colored molds, persistent over-gassing after weeks, or off flavors.
- Label: date, salt %, method (mash/brine), key ingredients.

G)Quick blueprints(smallbatch)

- **Classic Chile Mash Hot Sauce**
  - ✓ Chiles 1,000 g (2.2 lb) + salt 2.5% = 25 g (0.9 oz).
  - ✓ Ferment 7–14 d @ 64–68 °F / 18–20 °C.
  - ✓ Blend with 50–200 mL (1.7–6.8 fl oz) reserved brine to taste.
  - ✓ Mature 3–7 d (cool room) or 1–2 wks (fridge).
- **Fruit-Forward Brine Sauce (Pineapple+Chile)**
  - ✓ Pineapple 300 g (0.66 lb) + chiles 700 g (1.54 lb); cover with 2.5% brine.
  - ✓ Ferment 3–6 d. Blend; adjust with brine.
  - ✓ Mature in fridge 1–2 wks. No oil in primary.

6.2.1 CHILI SAUCES (5 RECIPES)

Basic gear: 1 L (≈1 qt) wide-mouthjarfor~1,000g(2.2lb)batches,weight/airlock, blender, funnel & woozy bottles.

Saltguide:2.5%mash(by produce weight) • 2.5%brine (25 g / 0.9 ozsaltper 1,000 mL/ 34floz water).

Headspace:⅜–¾ in(1–2cm).Temperature:64–68 °F(18–20°C).

Nooil inprimary;add citrusonlyatserving.

1)RED CHILI — METHOD: MASH (RECOMMENDED)

Ingredients(yields~24–30floz / 700–900mL)

- **Red chiles (Fresno/jalapeño/serrano mix), destemmed:** 1,000 g (2.2 lb)
- **Garlic:** 2–3 cloves (optional)
- **Salt:** 25 g (0.9 oz) (2.5%)

Step-by-Step

1.Prep (seed/derib partly for less heat).

2.Coarsely chop; mix in salt (and garlic).

3.Pack/press until self-brine appears; transfer to jar.

4.Add weight; airlock or daily burp (days 1–5).

5.Ferment7–14 days @ 64–68 °F; bubbles/haze = normal.

6.Blend smooth; thin with 2–8 Tbsp (30–120 mL / 1–4 fl oz) reserved brine.

7.Optional strain; optional 1–3 tsp (5–15 mL) 5% vinegar post-blend.

8.Mature 3–7 d cool room or 1–3 wks fridge.

9.Bottle (⅜–¾ in headspace) & refrigerate (4–8 wks).

Recommended Method

- **Standard:** Mash 7–14 d @ 64–68 °F.
- **Hybrid warm:** 12–24 h room →fridge 2–3 wks.
- **Cold-ferment:** fridge 3–4+ wks (gentler).

2)GREEN JALAPEÑO — METHOD: BRINE (RECOMMENDED FOR COLOR)

Ingredients(yields~24–30floz / 700–900mL)

- **Green jalapeños, thin rings:** 800 g (1.76 lb)
- **White onion, thin slices:** 100 g (0.22 lb) (optional)
- **Garlic**: 1 clove

  2.5% brine: make 1,000 mL (34 fl oz) water +25 g (0.9 oz) salt (use as needed to cover)

Step-by-Step

1.Slice (seed some for less heat).

2.Jar jalapeños + onion + garlic; cover with brine; leave headspace.

3.Add weight; airlock/burp daily.

4.Ferment5–10 days @ 64–68 °F (cool helps keep bright green).

5.Drain (reserve brine) & blend; thin with 2–10 Tbsp (30–150 mL / 1–5 fl oz) brine.

6.Optional strain; optional lime juice at serving and cilantro.

7.Mature 3–5 d cool room or 1–2 wks fridge; bottle & refrigerate.

Recommended Method

- **Standard:** Brine 5–8 d @ 64–68 °F.
- **Hybrid warm:** 12–24 h room →fridge 1–2 wks.
- **Cold-ferment:** fridge 2–3 wks (color & freshness max).

3)HABANERO-CARROT — METHOD: BRINE (RECOMMENDED)

Ingredients(yields~27–32floz / 800–950mL)

- **Carrots, ¼ in (½ cm) rounds:** 600 g (1.32 lb)
- **Orange habaneros, destemmed (whole or halved):** 400 g (0.88 lb)
- **Onion**: 50–80 g (0.11–0.18 lb) (optional) • Garlic: 2 cloves
- **2.5% brine:** 1,000 mL (34 fl oz) water + 25 g (0.9 oz) salt (as needed)

Step-by-Step

1.Prep carrots, habaneros (prick whole 2–3×), onion, garlic.

2.Pack in layers; cover with brine; weight on top.

3.Ferment6–9 days @ 64–68 °F; taste from day 5.

4.Drain (reserve brine) & blend smooth; add 1.7–6.8 fl oz (50–200 mL) brine to adjust.

5.Optional 1–2 tsp (5–10 mL) 5% vinegar or 1–2% honey after blending.

6.Mature 3–7 d cool room or 1–2 wks fridge; bottle & refrigerate.

Recommended Method

- **Standard:** Brine 6–9 d @ 64–68 °F (bright orange, clear heat).
- **Hybrid warm:** 12–24 h room →fridge 1–2 wks.
- **Cold-ferment:** fridge 2–3+ wks (softer heat).

4)FRESNO-GARLIC — METHOD: MASH (RECOMMENDED)

Ingredients (yields ~24–30 fl oz / 700–900 mL)

- **RedFresnochiles,destemmed:** 1,000 g (2.2 lb)
- **Garlic:** 4–5 cloves (12–20 g / 0.4–0.7 oz)
- **Salt:** 25g(0.9 oz) (2.5%)

Step-by-Step

1.Prep carrots, habaneros (prick whole 2–3×), onion, garlic.

2.Pack in layers; cover with brine; weight on top.

3.Ferment6–9 days @ 64–68 °F; taste from day 5.

4.Drain (reserve brine) & blend smooth; add 1.7–6.8 fl oz (50–200 mL) brine to adjust.

5.Optional 1–2 tsp (5–10 mL) 5% vinegar or 1–2% honey after blending.

6.Mature 3–7 d cool room or 1–2 wks fridge; bottle & refrigerate.

Recommended Method

- **Standard:** Mash 7–12 d @ 64–68 °F (rounded garlic, vivid red).
- **Hybrid warm**: 12–24 h room →fridge 2–3 wks.
- **Cold-ferment:** fridge 3–4 wks (gentler).

5)CHIPOTLE-TOMATO — METHOD: BRINE (RECOMMENDED)

Ingredients (yields ~27–34 fl oz / 800–1,000 mL)

- Ripe tomatoes, diced:800 g (1.76 lb)
- Dried chipotles, rehydrated: 20–25 g(0.7–0.9oz)
- Onion: 100 g (0.22 lb) • Garlic: 2 cloves
- 2.5% brine: 1,000 mL (34 fl oz) water + 25 g (0.9 oz)
- salt (as needed)

  (Optional) Dried oregano: ½ tsp

Step-by-Step

1.Rehydrate chipotles in hot water 10–15 min; drain (don't use unsalted soak water).

2.Jar tomatoes, onion, garlic, chipotles (and oregano); cover with brine; weight.

3.Ferment4–6 days @ 64–68 °F; taste from day 4.

4.Drain (reserve brine) & blend very smooth; add 1.7–6.8 fl oz (50–200 mL) brine to thin.

5.Optional 1–3 tsp (5–15 mL) 5% vinegar post-blend; optional strain for a silky sauce.

6.Mature 2–5 d cool room or 1–2 wks fridge; bottle & refrigerate.

Recommended Method

- **Standard:** Brine 4–6 d @ 64–68 °F (rounded smoke, bright red).
- **Hybrid warm:** 12–24 h room →fridge 1–2 wks.
- **Cold-ferment:** fridge 2–3 wks (softer smoke).

6.2.2 KETCHUP (1)

FERMENTED KETCHUP — METHOD: MASH/PURÉE (RECOMMENDED)

Gear: 1 L (≈1qt) wide-mouthjar,follower/weight(silicone disc or cabbage leaf), tamper/spoon, optional airlock, blender, funnel & woozy bottles.

Safetynote: no oil in the primaryferment.Use potent spices (clove/cinnamon) in low doses.

Ingredients(yields~25–30floz/ 750–900 mL)

- **Double-concentrated tomato paste:** 700 g (1.54 lb)
- **Water (to loosen):** 250 mL (8.5 fl oz)
- **Salt:** 2%oftotalmix → for ≈950 g total = 19 g (0.67 oz)
- **Classic spice profile**
  - **Onion powder:** 2 tsp (≈ 6 g / 0.21 oz)
  - **Garlic powder or 1 minced clove:** 1 tsp (≈ 3 g / 0.11 oz)
  - **Mustard powder:** ½ tsp (≈ 1 g / 0.04 oz)
  - **Sweet or smoked paprika (optional):** ½–1 tsp (≈ 1–2 g)
  - **Ground allspice:** ¼ tsp (≈ 0.5 g)
  - **Ground cinnamon:** ¼ tsp (≈ 0.5 g)
  - **Ground clove, pinch:** 1⁄16 tsp (≈ 0.1 g)

- **Post-ferment balancing (to taste, optional)**
  - **5% apple cider vinegar:** 15–30 mL (1–2 Tbsp)
  - **Brown sugar/honey/date syrup:** 20–30 g (0.7–1.1 oz) (~2–3% of sauce weight)
  - **(Optional) Xanthan gum:** 0.1–0.2% →1–2 g per 1,000 g sauce (0.04–0.07 oz per 2.2 lb)

Step-by-Step

1.Mix & salt

- Combine 700 g paste + 250 mL water until smooth & thick.
- Add 19 g (0.67 oz) salt (2%) and all spices; mix thoroughly.

2.Jar & level

- Transfer to a 1 L jar; smooth the surface to remove air pockets. Place a follower (silicone
- disc or cabbage leaf) and pour a thin "brine cap" of 2% brine over the top (only 2–3 Tbsp / 30–45 mL / 1–1.5 fl oz) to protect the surface.

3.Weight & close

- Add the weight; fit an airlock or burp once daily for the first 3–5 days.

4. Ferment

- 64–68 °F (18–20 °C) for 4–7 days.
- Normal: gentle bubbling, slight swell, clean tangy-tomato aroma.

5. Blend & adjust

- **Remove weight;** blend until silky. For thinner texture add water or reserved brine: 1–4 Tbsp (15–60 mL / 0.5–2 fl oz).
- **Balance (optional):** add vinegar and sweetener to taste.
- **(Optional) Stabilize:** blend in 0.1–0.2% xanthan to reduce separation.

6. Mature

- Move to a jar; with airlock or a slightly loose lid, let 3–5 days at 64–68 °F or 1–2 weeks in the fridge for flavor to knit.

7.Bottle & store

- Bottle with ⅜–¾ in (1–2 cm) headspace.
- Refrigerate: 4–8 weeks (often longer if clean and acidic). Shake before use.

Recommended Method

- **Standard (cool room):** 4–7 days primary @ 64–68 °F, then 3–5 days maturation.
- **Hybrid (warm climate):** 24 h room temp →fridge 1–2 weeks.
- **Cold-ferment:** fridge-only 3–4 weeks → very gentle, bright color.

Quick Variations (optional)

- **Smoky**: use smoked paprika (1 tsp) + 1 tsp (5 mL) malt vinegar post-ferment.
  Spicy: add ½–1 tsp red chili flakes or gochugaru to the initial mix.

6.2.3 MUSTARDS(2)

Basic gear: 1 L (≈1 qt) wide-mouth jar, weight/disc, optional airlock, optional fine sieve, blender/processor, funnel & jars/bottles.

Salt guide: 3% brine (e.g.,18 g / 0.6oz salt in 600 mL/ 20 floz water)tofully cover seeds.

Headspace: ¾–1 in (2–3 cm).Temperature: 64–68 °F (18–20 °C).

Safety: no oil in primary. Add vinegar/honey after ferment.

1)CLASSIC MUSTARD — METHOD: BRINE → BLEND

Ingredients (yields ~17–24 fl oz / 500–700 mL)

- **Yellow mustard seeds:** 200 g (7.1 oz)
- **Brown mustard seeds:** 100 g (3.5 oz)
- **3% brine:** prepare 600 mL (20 fl oz) water + 18 g (0.6 oz) salt (use as needed; keep extra ready)
- **Garlic:** 1 clove (optional)
- **Optional spices:** turmeric ½ tsp; freshly cracked black pepper ½ tsp
- **Post-blend (optional):** 5% apple cider or white wine vinegar 1–4 Tbsp (15–60 mL / 0.5–2 fl oz)

Step-by-Step

1.Rinse seeds under cold water.

2.Jar seeds (plus garlic/spices if using), then cover with 3% brine by at least ¾–1 in (2–3 cm).

3.Add weight; fit airlock (or burp daily for days 1–5).

4.**Ferment 5–7 days @ 64–68 °F.**

Normal: plumped seeds,gentle bubbling, sharpbut clean aroma.

5.Drain(reserve brine!) and blend: pulse for coarse style or blend longer for smooth.

Thin with 2–8 Tbsp (30–120 mL / 1–4 fl oz) reserved brine to desired texture.

6.Taste & balance (optional) with vinegar added gradually.

7.Mature: jar loosely capped or under airlock 1–3 days @ 64–68 °F, then refrigerate.

8.Store: 4–8 weeks in the fridge; heat stabilizes over 24–72 h.

Recommended Method

- **Standard (coolroom):** 5–7 d brine, then blend + 1–3 d maturation.
- **Hybrid (warmclimate):** 3–4 d room →fridge 3–5 d before blending.
- **Texture tip:** for extra smooth, sieve through a fine chinois after blending.

Heat control: adding vinegar later "locks" heat. Wait 24–48 h after blending before acidifying if you want a livelier kick.

2)HONEY MUSTARD — METHOD: BRINE → BLEND, SWEETENED POST-FERMENT

Ingredients (yields ~19–25 fl oz / 550–750 mL)

- **Yellow mustard seeds:** 200 g (7.1 oz) **Brown**
- **mustard seeds:** 100 g (3.5 oz) **3% brine:** 600 mL
- (20 fl oz) water + 18 g (0.6 oz) salt (as needed)
- (Optional) Turmeric ½ tsp • Cracked black pepper ¼–½ tsp

Post-blend

- ✓ Honey: 50–100 g (1.8–3.5 oz) (≈8–12% of
- ✓ sauce weight, to taste)
- ✓ 5% vinegar (ACV or white wine): 1–3 Tbsp
- ✓ (15–45 mL / 0.5–1.5 fl oz)

Step-by-Step

1. Ferment seeds exactly as in Classic Mustard (steps 1–4).
2. Drain & blend, thinning with 2–8 Tbsp (30–120 mL / 1–4 fl oz) reserved brine to texture.
3. Whisk in honey, tasting as you go; then balance with vinegar to your target sweet-tang.
4. Mature1–2 days @ 64–68 °F (loosely capped), then refrigerate.
5. Store4–8 weeks in the fridge; stir if natural separation occurs.

Recommended Method

- **Standard**: 5–7 d seed ferment; blend →honey + vinegar; 1–2 d maturation.
- **Sweetness guide:** 8–10% honey for sandwich spread; 12% for glazes.
- **Texture tip:** for coarse-grain, blend only half the seeds and fold in the rest whole/hydrated.

6.2.4 RELISHES (3)

Basic gear: 1 L (≈1 qt) wide-mouth jar, weight/disc, optional airlock, bowl, strainer, spoon/tamper.

Headspace: ¾–1 in (2–3 cm).Temperature: 64–68 °F(18–20 °C).

Rules:no oil in primary; tune juicinesswithreserved brine or self-brine.

Top-up: if needed, use2.5% brine (25 g / 0.9oz salt per 1,000 mL/ 34 floz water).

1)CUCUMBER RELISH — METHOD: DRY-SALT (RECOMMENDED), WITH OPTIONAL TOP-UP

Ingredients(yields~24–30floz / 700–900mL)

- **Firm pickling cucumbers, seeded if large, ¼–⅜ in(½–¾ cm)dice:** 800 g (1.76 lb)
- Sweet or red onion, fine dice: 150 g (0.33 lb)
- **Fresh dill, roughly chopped:** 10 g (0.35 oz)
- **Mustard seed or dill seed:** 1 tsp (≈ 2 g / 0.07 oz)
- **Salt:** 2.5% of total weight (e.g., 1,000 g → 25 g / 0.9 oz)
- (Optional, post-ferment "sweet relish") 5% vinegar 1–2 Tbsp (15–30 mL) + sugar10–20 g (0.35–0.7 oz)

Step-by-Step

1.Prep cukes: wash, peel if thick-skinned; halve & de-seed if large.

2.Dice cucumbers & onion evenly; add dill and seeds.

3.Salt at 2.5% (use 3% in warm rooms): mix 1–2 min →rest 15–30 min → massage 1–2 min until self-brine forms.

4.Pack & press into the jar; target ⅜–¾ in (1–2 cm) liquid above. If short, add a few Tbsp of 2.5% brine.

5.Add weight; fit airlock or burp daily (days 1–5).

6.Ferment3–5 days @ 64–68 °F; taste from day 3.

7.Refrigerate; optionally balance "sweet relish" style with vinegar + sugar after ferment.

8.Store3–5 weeks in the fridge. Stir before serving.

Recommended Method

- **Standard:** 3–5 d @ 64–68 °F (high crunch).
- **Hybrid warm:** 12–24 h room →fridge 1–2 wks.
- **Cold-ferment:** fridge 2–3 wks for maximum crispness.

2) SWEETCORN & JALAPEÑO RELISH — METHOD: BRINE (RECOMMENDED)

Ingredients(yields~27–32floz / 800–950mL)

- **Fresh corn kernels (raw, cut from cob):** 700g (1.54 lb)
- **Jalapeño, fine dice (seeded for less heat):** 120 g (0.26 lb)
- **Red onion, diced:** 150 g (0.33 lb)
- **Garlic**: 1 clove, minced
- **2.5% brine:** make1,000mL(34floz)water+25 g (0.9 oz) salt (use as needed to cover)
- (**Optional) Lime zest;** cilantro at serving

Step-by-Step

1. Cut kernels; dice jalapeño & onion.
2. Jar corn + jalapeño + onion + garlic; cover with 2.5% brine leaving ¾–1 in (2–3 cm) headspace; add weight.
3. Ferment3–6 days @ 64–68 °F (corn sugars speed up). Taste from day 3.
4. Drain (reserve brine); adjust juiciness by adding 1–4 Tbsp (15–60 mL / 0.5–2 fl oz) brine to taste.
5. Optional lime zest now; cilantro only at serving.
6. Refrigerate; best within 3–5 weeks.

Recommended Method

- **Standard:** 3–5d @ 64–68 °F (bright sweet-tang).
- **Hybrid warm:** 12–24 h room →fridge 1–2 wks.
- **Cold-ferment:** fridge 2–3 wks for vivid crunch & color.

3) ONION-PEPPER RELISH — METHOD: DRY-SALT (RECOMMENDED)

Ingredients (yields ~19–25 fl oz / 550–750 mL)

- Red onion, ⅛–¼ in (¼–½ cm) dice: 500 g (1.10 lb)
- Sweet bell peppers (red/yellow), diced: 450 g (0.99 lb)
- Jalapeño or serrano, fine dice: 50 g (0.11 lb)
- Mustard or celery seed: 1 tsp (≈ 2 g / 0.07 oz)
- Salt: 2% of total weight (1,000 g → 20 g / 0.7 oz) (Optional, post-ferment "light chow-chow") 5%
- vinegar 2–6 tsp (10–30 mL) + sugar 10–20 g (0.35–0.7 oz)

Step-by-Step

1. Even dice onion & peppers; add chile and seeds.
2. Salt at 2%: mix 1–2 min →rest 20–30 min →massage 1–2 min to build self-brine.
3. Pack & press; ensure ⅜–¾ in (1–2 cm) brine above (top up with 2% brine if needed: 20 g salt per 1,000 mL / 34 fl oz).
4. Add weight; airlock or daily burp 3–5 days.
5. Ferment5–7 days @ 64–68 °F; taste from day 5.
6. Refrigerate; optionally balance with vinegar + sugar after ferment.
7. Store4–6 weeks in the fridge.

Recommended Method

- **Standard:** 5–7 d @ 64–68 °F (crunch & vivid color).
- **Hybrid warm:** 12–24 h room →fridge 1–2 wks.
- **Cold-ferment:** fridge 2–3 wks for gentler profile.

6.2.5 FRESH “FRIDGE” TOMATO SAUCE (1)

FRESH “FRIDGE”TOMATOSAUCE

Method: Mash (dry-salt) with fridge maturation

Gear: 1 L(≈1 qt)wide-mouthjar,weight/disc, optional airlock, strainer,blender/immersion, funnel & jars/bottles.

Headspace: ¾–1 in (2–3 cm).

Safety: no oil in primary. Add freshbasil after ferment tokeep it bright green.

Ingredients (yields ~24–30 fl oz / 700–900 mL)

- **Firm ripe tomatoes (Roma/plum),** ½ in (1 cm) dice, seed/gel removed if very watery: 1,000 g (2.2 lb)
  Sweet onion, fine dice: 80–100 g (0.18–0.22 lb) (optional)
- **Garlic:** 1–2 cloves, finely minced (optional)
  Red chili flakes or black pepper: ¼–½ tsp (optional)
- **Salt:** 2% of total weight →20 g (0.7 oz) for 1,000 g
- **(Optional, post-ferment)** Fresh basil 10–15 g (0.35–0.53 oz) • 5% vinegar1–3 tsp (5–15 mL) to round

Recommended Method (quick view)

- **Standard**:2–3d@64–68°F →blend → fridge.
- **Hybrid warm:** 12–24 h room →fridge 3–5 d → blend.
- **Cold-ferment:** 5–10 d fridge-only → blend (max fresh color/notes).

Step-by-Step

1.Prep tomatoes

- Destem, halve, spoon out seeds/gel if watery; pat excess moisture. Dice ½ in (1 cm).

2.Salt & macerate (self-brine)

- Toss tomatoes(+ onion/garlic/spices if using) with 20 g (0.7 oz) salt (2%).
- Mix 1–2 min, then rest 15–30 min to draw self-brine.

3.Pack & press

- Pack intoa1 L (≈1 qt) jar, press firmly so liquid covers solids by ⅜–¾ in (1–2 cm).
- Add weight; keep ¾–1 in (2–3 cm) headspace.
- If short on liquid: top up with 2% brine (20 g / 0.7 oz saltper 1,000 mL / 34 fl oz water) just to cover.

4. Ferment

- **Standard(fresh, lightly tangy):** 2–3 days at 64–68 °F (18–20 °C); taste daily.
- Hybrid (warm rooms/bright color): 12–24 h at 64–68 °F, then fridge 3–5 days.
- **Cold-ferment (max freshness):** 5–10 days in the fridge only (gentler acid, vibrant color).
  Normal: light bubbling, clean tomato/lactic aroma.

5. Drain if needed & blend

- Ifvery juicy,strain(reserve liquid). Blend raw to desired smoothness. Thin with reserved self-brine:
- 1–4 Tbsp (15–60 mL / 0.5–2 fl oz).
  For a silkier passata, sieve after blending.

6.Finish (post-ferment)

- Fold in freshbasil and, if desired, 1–3 tsp (5–15 mL) 5% vinegar. No oil yet; add at serving.

7.Brief maturation & storage

- Bottle/jar and refrigerateimmediately;let flavors knit 24–48 h in the fridge.
  Keeps 2–3 weeksrefrigerated. Stir beforeuse; discardif odd smells,colored molds,or persistent foaming.

6.2.6 BLACK GARLIC (1) – HOME PROCESS NOTES

What it is: Black garlic is not lactic fermentation. It's a low-heat, high-humidity aging that triggers early enzymatic change and then Maillard reactions, converting sugars & amino acids.

Process target: 149–167 °F (65–75 °C) at high humidity 70–90% RH for 2–6 weeks, without drying or cooking the bulbs hard.

Home equipment (pick one)

- Rice cooker / slow cooker with a stable "keep warm" at 149–167 °F (65–75 °C) (verify with a probe thermometer).
- Dehydrator with temp control up to 158–167 °F (70–75 °C), a closed chamber (plastic bin) and a water pan for humidity.
- Bread proofer capable of 158 °F (70 °C) with humidity control.

Odor: the aromais strong. Run the devicein a ventilated area (garage/covered balcony).

Raw material

- Whole heads, tight skins, no
- mold, no sprouting.
  Don't wash; brush off dirt; keep skins on.

Step-by-step (batches of 8–20 heads)

1. **Verify temp & set up**

- ☑ Preheat the empty unit 1–2 h and measure: aim for 149–167 °F (65–75 °C), steady.
- ☑ Add a water pan for humidity and a rack to keep garlic off the floor of the unit.

2.Prep heads

- Trim only the root fuzz flush. Do not break the head; keep skins intact.

3.Wrap to retain moisture (optional but helpful)

- Wrap each head loosely in parchment then foil, or place in a thick paper bag.
- Avoid plastics for long hot holds.

4.Load & start

- Arrange a single layer on the rack. Add the water pan.
- Set 158 °F (70 °C) if available; otherwise use a verified warm-hold.

5.Long run (2–6 weeks)

- Keep temp/humidity continuous. Daily checks:
- Water in the pan; top up as needed.
- Condensation; wipe drips that might wet bulbs.
- Color/odor: amber (days 5–10) →brown (week 2) →jet black (weeks 3–5).
- Electrical safety: proper outlet, intact cord, stable surface; don't block vents.

6.Doneness tests

- Cloves uniformly black, translucent, sticky-soft (like a prune).
- Taste: sweet-sour, balsamic,
- licorice/soy/molasses notes; no burnt bitterness.
- If dry/chalky→ too hot/too dry: add humidity, drop a few °F/°C, continue 3–7 days.
- If still brown & sharp → needs more time: continue 3–10 days and recheck.

7. Condition (rest)

- Power off; cool 12–24 h at room temp.
- For best texture, hold bulbs 2–7 days sealed at 64–68 °F (18–20 °C) to let flavors meld.

8. Storage

- **Whole, unpeeled:** refrigerate 1–3 months (vac-seal or well-sealed, dry).
- **Peeled**: refrigerate 2–4 weeks with a dry paper towel in the container.
- **Freeze**: 6–12 months (peeled cloves or puree in portions).
- **Important**: no oil at room temp. Garlic + oil must be refrigerated and used within 7 days.

Quick troubleshooting

- Hard/dry cloves → raise humidity, drop to 149–155 °F (65–68 °C), extend time. Bitter/burnt→ temp too high; reduce 5–9 °F (3–5 °C). Visible mold before blackening → chamber too cool/stagnant. Discard affected bulbs, sanitize, restart at correct temp. House odor → run unit in vented area or place inside a secondary box with a small carbon filter.

Use ideas

- Paste (cloves + 1–2 tsp / 5–10 mL water) to finish risottos, aioli, pan sauces.
- Powder (dry at 122 °F / 50 °C, grind) for rubs, popcorn, eggs.
- Whole cloves on cheese boards, steaks, roast veg.

6.2.7 BRINE REUSE (3)

What "brine" means here: the acidic liquid from your lactic ferments (pickles, onions, krauts).

Safety & quality

- Use only brines from successful ferments: no colored molds, fresh sour aroma, no sliminess.
- Keep brine refrigerated at all times.
- Oil + brine mixes must be refrigerated and used within 7–10 days (clean utensils).
- Optional: typical pH ≈3.5–4.2; lower = sharper tang.

1)PICKLE-BRINE VINAIGRETTE

Step-by-Step

1. In a jar, combine brine + mustard (and honey). Shake 10 sec.
2. Add oil in a thin stream; shake vigorously 20–30 sec to emulsify.
3. Fold in shallot/herbs; taste and adjust salt/pepper.
4. Rest 10 min; shake before serving.

Storage: 7–10 days in the fridge (oil may solidify; warm briefly & shake).

Use: leafy salads, potato salads, quick marinades, grain bowls.

Ingredients (yields ~8.5 fl oz / 250 mL)

- Oil (extra-virgin olive or neutral): 5.4 fl oz (160 mL)
- Ferment brine (e.g., dill pickle): 2.7 fl oz (80 mL)
- Dijon mustard: 2 tsp (10 mL)
- (Optional) Honey or maple: 2 tsp (10 mL)
- (Optional) Minced shallot: 0.5 oz (15 g)
- Black pepper: ¼ tsp
- Salt to taste (often not needed)
- (Optional) Fresh dill, chopped: ½ heaped tsp (≈2 g)

Recommended Method

Base ratio 2:1 (oil:brine). For brighter tang use 3:2; for lighter body use 1:1.

2)BRINE MAYO DIP

Ingredients (yields ~10 fl oz / 300 mL)

- Mayonnaise (store-bought or proper homemade): 1 cup (240 mL)
- Ferment brine: 2–4 Tbsp (30–60 mL / 1–2 fl oz)
- Dijon mustard: 1 tsp (5 mL)
- Garlic powder: ¼ tsp
- (Optional) Chopped gherkins/capers: 0.5 oz (15 g)
- (Optional) Dill or chives, chopped: 1–2 tsp

Recommended Method

Start with 2 Tbsp (30 mL) brine; increase to 4 Tbsp(60 mL) for a lighter,tangier dip.

Step-by-Step

1.Whisk mayo + mustard + garlic powder.

2.Add brine by tablespoons to a creamy, scoopable texture.

3.Fold in pickles/capers and herbs.

4.Chill at least 1 hour to meld.

Storage: 5–7 days refrigerated.

Use: fries, crudités, sandwiches, potato/coleslaw dressing.

3)BRINE BLOODY-MARY BASE

Ingredients (yields ~34floz/1.0L,non-alcoholic base — add spirits at serving)

- **Tomato juice:** 25floz(750mL)
- **Ferment brine (spicy or dill):** 4 fl oz (120 mL)
- **Fresh lemon juice:** 1floz(30mL / 2 Tbsp)
- **Worcestershire:** 1Tbsp(15mL) (contains anchovy;
- **veg option:** soysauceorvegan Worcestershire)
- **Prepared horseradish:** 1Tbsp (15 g / 0.5 oz)
- **Fermented hot sauce** (see6.2.1): 1–2 tsp (5–10 mL)
- **Celery salt:** ½ tsp
- **Black pepper:** ¼ tsp
- **(Optional) Smoked paprika**:¼ tsp

Step-by-Step

1. Whisk all ingredients in a pitcher until smooth.
2. Taste; adjust heat/acidity with brine or hot sauce.
3. Chill 2–24 hours to meld.

Serving (optional alcohol): per 8 fl oz (240 mL) base, add 1.5 fl oz (45 mL) vodka over ice. Garnish with celery stick, lemon wedge, and a pickle.

Storage: base keeps 3–4 days in the fridge. Shake before pouring.

Recommended Method

Use spicy brines for complexity; if too salty, dilute with tomato juice to about 4:1 (tomato:brine).

CHAPTER 7

FERMENTED FRUIT & HOME VINEGARS (10 RECIPES)

7.1 METHODS & STEP-BY-STEP PROCEDURES

7.1.1 NATURAL SUGARS • SPICES • PRESSURE MANAGEMENT • STARTING VINEGARS

Basic gear

- 1–2 qt (1–2 L) wide-mouth jars with weights and (for fruit) airlocks; cloth + band for vinegars.
- Scale, funnel, fine strainer/cheesecloth, woozy bottles.
- Optional pH strips/meter; optional hydrometer/refractometer.
- Use glass/food-grade; no reactive metals with acids.

A)Pick your process

1.Lacto-fruit — quick tang, bright fruit.

✓ Salt:2.0–2.5%bytotal weight (mash)or2.0–3.0%brine.

✓ 64–68 °F (18–20 °C) for 3–7 days, then refrigerate.

2.Home vinegar (two stages) — stable pantry staple.

✓ Alcoholic stage first,thenacetic stage withAcetobacter.

✓ Starter:add 10–20%v/v raw,unpasteurized vinegar ora vinegar mother.

Safety: no oil in ferments; bottle acidic liquids only once stable (typical vinegar pH ≈2.4–3.5).

B) Natural sugars: how much

- Sweeter fruits ferment faster.
- For the alcoholic stage: rule of thumb →~17 g sugar per liter ≈ 1% ABV.

✓ Example: target ~6% ABV →~100 g/L sugar (3.5 oz/qt).

✓ Sources: table sugar, brown sugar, honey (slower), fruit juice.

For lacto-fruit:noadded sugar;rely on2.0–2.5%salt (use3%in warmrooms).

C) Spices

- Clove, cinnamon, bay, juniper can inhibit microbes → go light (≤ 0.5–1.0% of fruit weight; e.g., 2–5 g / 0.07–0.18 oz per 500 g / 1.1 lb).
- Lacto-fruit: whole spices in tiny amounts.

Vinegars: best post-acid infusion during maturation.

D) Pressure management (CO_2)

- Lacto-fruit: airlock or daily burp first 3–5 days; ¾–1 in (2–3 cm) headspace.
- Alcoholic stage: airlock; leave 15–20% headspace.
- Acetic stage: no airlock; needs oxygen. Cover with cloth.
- Never bottle sweet/active liquids in sealed glass: explosion risk. Chill & waitfor stability.

E)Starters for vinegars (practical)

- Raw ACV with the mother: add 10–20% v/v to alcoholic base → lowers pH, seeds Acetobacter.
- Vinegar mother: place gently on top; avoid heavy agitation.
- Kombucha SCOBY: can acidify, but raw vinegar starter yields cleaner fruit vinegars.
- Air exchange: wide mouth vessels, 75–86 °F (24–30 °C) speed acetic work.

F)Core blueprints

F1) Lacto-fruit in brine (1 qt / ≈1 L)

Ingredients

- ✓ Fruit pieces: 28–32 oz (800–900 g)
- ✓ 2.5% brine: 0.9 oz (25 g) salt in 34 fl oz (1,000 mL) water (use just to cover)
- ✓ (Optional) Whole spices 0.04–0.11 oz (1–3 g) total

Steps

1. Jar fruit; add minimal spices.
2. Cover with 2.5% brine; ¾–1 in (2–3 cm) headspace; add weight.
3. Ferment3–6 days @ 64–68 °F (18–20 °C); taste from day 3.
4. Refrigerate; enjoy within 2–4 weeks.

In warm rooms use 3% salt or switch to fridge after 12–24 h.

Normal vs not

- **Normal**: fine bubbles, yogurt-fruit aroma.
- **Not**: colored molds, solvent/rotten odors →discard.

F2) Fruit "wine" → Vinegar (2.1 qt / 2 L batch)

Alcoholic stage (with airlock)

- Raw ACV with the mother: add 10–20% v/v to alcoholic base → lowers pH, seeds Acetobacter.
- Vinegar mother: place gently on top; avoid heavy agitation.
- Kombucha SCOBY: can acidify, but raw vinegar starter yields cleaner fruit vinegars.
- Air exchange: wide mouth vessels, 75–86 °F (24–30 °C) speed acetic work.

Steps

1. Mix fruit/juice + water + dissolved sugar.
2. Fit airlock; 64–72 °F (18–22 °C) for 5–10 days until bubbling subsides.

Acetic stage (open to air)

- Add raw vinegar 10–20% v/v (7–14 fl oz / 200–400 mL).
- Wide-mouth vessel, cloth cover.
- 75–86 °F (24–30 °C) for 3–8 weeks.
- A surface mother is normal. Taste weekly; when bright and clean, strain and bottle.

Mature & store

- Rest 2–4 weeks (loosely capped to vent any CO_2), then cap fully.
- Cool, dark storage. Target acidity 4–6% (typical pH 2.4–3.5).

F3) "Express vinegar" (from ready wine/cider)

- Use unsulfited wine/cider 34 fl oz (1.0 L).
- Add 3.4–6.8 fl oz (100–200 mL) raw vinegar (10–20%).
- Wide mouth + cloth, 75–82 °F (24–28 °C) for 2–6 weeks → done.
- Ideal for post-acid spice infusions 3–7 days, then strain.

7.2.1 FERMENTED FRUIT (6 RECIPES)

Basic gear: 1 qt (≈1 L) wide-mouth jar, weight/disc, optional airlock, funnel, strainer.

Salt guide: 2.5% brine (e.g., 0.9 oz / 25 g salt in 34 fl oz / 1,000 mL water) — use 3% in warm rooms.

Headspace: ¾–1 in (2–3 cm). Temperature: 64–68 °F (18–20 °C).

Top-up: add 2.5% brine (or 3% warm rooms) just to cover the fruit.

Safety:nooil; burp daily if no airlock. Sweet fruits = short timelines.

1)CINNAMON APPLES — METHOD: BRINE

Ingredients (1 qt / ≈1 L; yields ~24–30 fl oz / 700–900 mL)

- Crisp apples, ½ in (1–1.5 cm) dice, cored: 1.98 lb (900 g)
- Cinnamon stick: 1 small (0.07–0.11 oz / 2–3 g)
- (Optional) Lemon zest (no pith): from ½ lemon 2.5% brine to cover (keep 34 fl oz / 1,000 mL ready)

Step-by-Step

1.Prep apples; dice evenly.

2.Jar apples + cinnamon (+ zest); add weight.

3.Cover with 2.5% brine; ¾–1 in headspace.

4.Ferment3–5 days @ 64–68 °F; taste from day 3.

5.Refrigerate; enjoy within 2–4 weeks.

Recommended Method

- **Standard**:3–4d (crisp + light tang).
- **Warm rooms:** 3% salt or 12–24 h room → fridge 3–5 d.
- **Cold-ferment:** fridge 5–7 d for max crunch.

2)SPICED PEARS — METHOD: BRINE

Ingredients (1 qt / ≈1 L)

- Firm pears, ½ in (1–1.5 cm) wedges, cored: 1.98 lb (900 g)
- Star anise: 1 (≈ 0.04 oz / 1 g)
- Vanilla (seeds or a 1–1½ in / 3–4 cm piece of pod): small
- (Optional) Fresh ginger matchsticks: 0.35 oz (10 g)
- 2.5% brine to cover

Step-by-Step

1.Slice pears; add anise, vanilla (and ginger).

2.Cover with 2.5% brine; weight; ¾–1 in headspace.

3.Ferment 3–5 days; taste day 3–4.

4.Refrigerate; best 2–4 weeks.

Recommended Method

- **Standard**:3–5d; soft spice, firm fruit.
- **Warm rooms:** 3% salt or 12–24 h room →fridge.
- **Cold-ferment:** fridge 5–8 d for extra snap.

3) TEPACHE-STYLE PINEAPPLE — METHOD: SPICED BRINE

Ingredients(1qt / ≈1L)

- Ripe but firm pineapple, ½ in (1–1.5 cm) dice: 1.98 lb (900 g)
- Cinnamon stick: 1 small (0.07–0.11 oz / 2–3 g) Allspice berries or cloves: 2–3 total (≤0.02 oz / 0.5 g)
- (Optional, post-ferment) Piloncillo/brown sugar 0.35–0.7 oz (10–20 g) to glaze
- 2.5% brine to cover

Step-by-Step

1. Trim/peel pineapple; dice.
2. Jar with spices; add weight.
3. Cover with 2.5% brine; ¾–1 in headspace.
4. Ferment2–4 days (sweet fruit ferments fast); taste from day 2.
5. Refrigerate; optional stir in 10–20 g piloncillo cold for tepache-like notes. Use within 2–3 weeks.

Recommended Method

- **Standard**:2–3d bright & tropical.
- **Warm rooms:** 3% salt or 12 h room → fridge 2–4 d.
- **Cold-ferment:** fridge 4–7 d (vivid color, gentle fizz).

4)MIXED BERRIES — METHOD: SHORT BRINE, COLD PREFERRED

Ingredients (1 qt / ≈1 L)

- Strawberries halved, blueberries whole, raspberries/blackberries whole: 1.87–1.98 lb (850–900 g)
- (Optional) Lemon zest threads
- 2.75–3% brine to cover (higher salt = better structure)

Step-by-Step

1. Dry-clean berries (no soaking); cut only strawberries.
2. Jar gently; add weight.
3. Cover with 2.75–3% brine; ¾–1 in headspace.
4. Ferment1–3 days @ 64–68 °F or cold-ferment 4–6 days in fridge.

Recommended Method

Cold-ferment favored for structure and color.

Standard: 1–2 d at room temp for extra sparkle.

Handle gently—raspberries are delicate.

5)GRAPES & ROSEMARY – METHOD: BRINE

Ingredients(1qt / ≈1L)

- Seedless grapes (firm, red or white): 1.98 lb (900 g)
- Fresh rosemary: 1 tiny tip (~0.04 oz / 1 g)
- (Optional) Cracked black pepper, 4–6 corns
- 2.5% brine to cover

Step-by-Step

1. Wash/dry grapes; keep whole.
2. Jar grapes + rosemary (+ pepper); add weight.
3. Cover with 2.5% brine; ¾–1 in headspace.
4. Ferment 3–5 days; taste day 3.
5. Refrigerate; keeps 2–4 weeks.

Recommended Method

- Standard: 3–4 d.
- Warm rooms: 3% salt or early move to fridge.
- Use rosemary sparingly (can dominate).

Normal vs not (all recipes)

- **Normal**: fine bubbles, slight haze, bright yogurt-fruit aroma; fruit fully submerged.
- **Not**: colored/fuzzy molds, rotten/solvent odors, slimy texture → discard.

6)PEACH-GINGER – METHOD: BRINE

Ingredients (1 qt / ≈1 L)

- Firm peaches (not over-ripe), ½ in (1–1.5 cm) wedges: 1.98 lb (900 g)
- Fresh ginger matchsticks: 0.35–0.53 oz (10–15 g)
- (Optional) Red chili flakes: ⅛ tsp
- 2.75–3% brine to cover

Step-by-Step

1. Peel if skins are tough; wedge; add ginger (and flakes).
2. Cover with 2.75–3% brine; weight; ¾–1 in headspace.
3. Ferment2–4 days; taste from day 2.
4. Refrigerate; best within 1–3 weeks.

Recommended Method

- **Standard**: 2–3 d to keep flesh firm.
- **Cold-ferment:** 4–7 d fridge-only for a gentler profile.
- **Warm rooms:** prefer 3% brine.

7.2.2 VINEGARS (3 RECIPES)

Basic gear: 1 qt (≈1 L) wide-mouth jar, breathable cloth/cheesecloth, rubber band or string, funnel, strainer.

Starter sugars: 1–2 tbsp (15–30 g) sugar per 34 fl oz / 1,000 mL water.

Headspace: ¾–1 in (2–3 cm). Temperature: 68–77 °F (20–25 °C).

Timeline: 2–3 weeks for alcohol stage + 3–4 weeks for acetic stage.

Safety: stir daily; discard surface molds immediately; final pH should reach 3.0–3.5 for culinary use.

1) APPLE-SCRAP VINEGAR — METHOD: NATURAL FERMENTATION

Ingredients (1 qt / ≈1L;yields~24–30fl oz / 700–900 mL)

- Apple peels and cores (organic/unwaxed): 1.98 lb (900 g)
- Filtered water: enough to cover
- Sugar: 1.5–2 tbsp (20–25 g)

Step-by-Step

- Collect apple scraps; place in jar.
- Add water + sugar; stir well.
- Cover with cloth; secure with rubber band.
- Stir daily; after 2–3 weeks strain out solids.
- Continue fermenting 3–4 more weeks until strong vinegar aroma develops.

Recommended Method

- **Standard:** 6–7 weeks total at 68–77 °F (20–25 °C).
- **Warm rooms:** reduce sugar; stir twice daily.
- **Cold rooms:** may take up to 8–9 weeks.

2)PINEAPPLE VINEGAR — METHOD: NATURAL FERMENTATION

Ingredients(1qt / ≈1L)

- Pineapple peel + core (ripe, firm): 1.98 lb (900 g)
- Filtered water: enough to cover
- Brown sugar: 2 tbsp (30 g)

Step-by-Step

- Place pineapple scraps in jar.
- Add water + sugar; stir.
- Cover with cloth; secure.
- Stir daily; alcohol aroma appears in 5–7 days.
- Strain and continue fermenting 3–4 weeks until sour.

Recommended Method

- **Standard:** 4–5 weeks total.
- **Warm rooms:** extra sugar speeds fermentation (watch for mold).
- **Cold rooms:** 6–7 weeks, slower but stable.

3) BERRY VINEGAR — METHOD: NATURAL FERMENTATION

Ingredients(1qt / ≈1L)

- Mixedberries (blueberries, blackberries, raspberries, strawberries): 1.87–1.98 lb (850–900 g)
- Filtered water: enough to cover
  Sugar (white or brown): 2 tbsp (30 g)
- (Optional) Fresh herbs: rosemary or thyme, 1 sprig

Step-by-Step

- Lightlycrush berries; place in jar.
- Add water + sugar; stir.
- Cover with cloth; secure.
- Stir daily for 5–7 days; then strain.
- Ferment liquid 3–4 more weeks until acidic.

Recommended Method

- Standard: 5–6 weeks total.
- Warm rooms: fast ferment, higher mold risk → stir often.
- Cold rooms: 7–8 weeks; milder flavor.

Normal vs Not Normal (all recipes)

- Normal:gentlefizz,sedimentatbottom, fruity-acid aroma.
- Not normal: fuzzy/colored mold, rotten/solvent smell → discard.

7.2.3 DESSERT-STYLE (1 RECIPE)

Basic gear: 1 qt (≈1 L) wide-mouth jar, weight/disc, optional airlock, funnel, strainer.

Salt guide: 2.5% brine (0.9 oz / 25 g salt in 34 fl oz / 1,000 mL water).

Headspace: ¾–1 in (2–3 cm). Temperature: 64–68 °F (18–20 °C).

Timeline: 2–3 days for sweet fruits; taste from day 2.

Safety: no oil; sweet + spice ferments move quickly → monitor closely.

1) VANILLA APPLE SLICES TOPPING — METHOD: BRINE

Ingredients(1qt / ≈1L;yields~24–30floz / 700–900mL)

- Crisp apples, sliced ½ in (1–1.5 cm) thick, cored: 1.98 lb (900 g)
- Vanilla bean: 1 piece (1–1½ in / 3–4 cm) or scraped seeds
- (Optional) Cinnamon stick: 0.07–0.11 oz (2–3 g)
- 2.5% brine to cover

Step-by-Step

1.Slice apples evenly.

2.Place slices in jar with vanilla (and cinnamon if used).

3.Cover with 2.5% brine; add weight.

4.Leave ¾–1 in headspace; ferment 2–3 days @ 64–68 °F.

5.Taste from day 2; refrigerate when flavor reaches desired tang.

Recommended Method

- **Standard:** 2–3 days → fresh, lightly tart, vanilla aroma.
- **Warm rooms:** 3% brine; refrigerate within 48 h.
- **Cold ferment:** 3–5 days in fridge → firmer, subtler topping.

Serving suggestion:

- Use as a topping for yogurt, ice cream, pancakes, or cheesecake; also excellent as a quick tart filling.

Normal vs Not Normal (all recipes)

- **Normal:** fine bubbles, sweet-spiced aroma, bright color.
- **Not normal:** fuzzy/colored mold, solvent odors, mushy texture → discard.

CHAPTER 8

DAIRY & PLANT-BASED ALTERNATIVES (12 RECIPES)

8.1 METHODS & STEP-BY-STEP PROCEDURES

8.1.1 STARTERS (YOGURT/KEFIR), INCUBATION, STRAINING, DAIRY & PLANT VARIANTS

Basic Starters

- **Yogurt**:begin with 2–3 tbsp plain natural yogurt (no additives) or freeze-dried lactic cultures.
- **Kefir**: requires kefir "grains," a living symbiotic colony of bacteria and yeasts that feed on lactose.

Incubation

- **Ideal temperature:** 104–110 °F (40–43 °C) for yogurt; 68–77 °F (20–25 °C) for kefir.
- **Time**:yogurt6–12 h → longer = tangier and thicker; kefir 18–36 h at room temp.
- **Containers**:glass or stainless steel; avoid thin plastics or aluminum.

Straining

- **Strained yogurt** = Greek-style: 4–12 h in fridge using cheesecloth or nut-milk bag.
- **Thick kefir:** drain 2–4 h; longer → cream-cheese-like spread.
- **Whey use:** excellent in marinades, drinks, or as a starter for other ferments.

Variants

- **Dairy**:wholecow'smilk = creamy texture; goat/sheep milk = stronger flavor.
- **Plant-based:**
  - **Soy milk:** bestoption for vegan yogurt (protein content supports culture).
  - **Coconut milk**:richand creamy, but benefits from natural thickeners (agar, tapioca).
  - **Oat/almond milk:** ferments slower; use tailored starter cultures.

Safety & practical notes

- All milk (animal or plant) should be boiled and cooled to inoculation temp unless already sterilized/UHT.
- Clean tools = safe fermentation.
- Avoid soap or chlorine residues (they inhibit cultures).

8.2.1 DAIRY (6 RECIPES)

1) PLAIN YOGURT – METHOD: INCUBATION

Ingredients (1 qt / ≈1L;yields~28–30fl oz / 850–900 mL)

- Whole cow's milk: 1 qt (≈1 L)
- Plain yogurt (starter): 2–3 tbsp (30–45 g)

Step-by-Step

- Heatmilk to near boil (≈185 °F / 85 °C); hold 5 min.
- Cool to 108–110 °F (42–43 °C).
- Add starter; stir gently.
- Incubate 6–10 h at 104–110 °F (40–43 °C).
- Refrigerate; thickens further after 12 h.

Recommended Method

- **Standard**: 8 h → mild and creamy.
- **Longer**: 10–12 h → tangier and firmer.
- **Use**: base for sweets, dressings, or fermented drinks.

2) HONEY-VANILLA YOGURT – METHOD: INCUBATION

Ingredients(1qt / ≈1L)

- Whole cow's milk:1 qt (≈1 L)
- Plain yogurt (starter): 2–3 tbsp (30–45 g)
- Vanilla bean (seeds): 1
- Rawhoney: 2–3 tbsp (40–60 g, post-ferment)

Step-by-Step

- Prepare like plain yogurt, adding vanilla seeds to warm milk.
- Incubate 6–10 h.
- Oncecooled, stirinhoney.

Recommended Method

Standard: 8 h →sweet,aromatic.

Storage: 5–7 days in fridge.

3) PLAIN MILK KEFIR – METHOD: NATURAL FERMENTATION

Ingredients(1qt / ≈1L)

- Whole cow's milk: 1 qt (≈1 L)
- Kefir grains: 2–3 tbsp (30–45 g)

Step-by-Step

- Place grains in milk at room temp.
- Cover with cloth; ferment 18–24 h @ 68–72 °F (20–22 °C).
- Strain grains with sieve; transfer to fresh milk.
- Drink immediately or refrigerate.

Recommended Method

- **Standard**: 24 h → lightly fizzy, tangy.
- **Longer**: 36 h → thicker, sharper.

4) CINNAMON KEFIR – METHOD: NATURAL FERMENTATION

Ingredients(1qt / ≈1L)

Whole cow's milk: 1 qt (≈1 L) Kefir grains: 2–3 tbsp (30–45 g) Small cinnamon stick: 1 (≈0.07–0.11 oz / 2–3 g)

Step-by-Step

Place grains + cinnamon in milk.

Cover; ferment 18–24 h @ 68–72 °F.

Strain grains; remove cinnamon.

Refrigerate; serve chilled.

Recommended Method

Standard: 24 h→mildspiced flavor.

Note: do not ferment >24 h with cinnamon (can turn bitter).

5) LABNEH WITH ZA'ATAR – METHOD: YOGURT STRAINING

Ingredients(yields~14–16oz / 400–450g

- Whole plain yogurt: 1 qt (≈1 L)
- Fine salt: ½ tsp (3 g)
- Za'atar spice blend: 1 tbsp (10 g)
- Extra virgin olive oil: to drizzle

Step-by-Step

- Mixyogurtwith salt.
- Strain 12–24 h in fridge with cheesecloth.
- Shape into balls or keep as thick cream.
- Serve with za'atar + olive oil.

Recommended Method

- **Standard**: 18–24 h → spreadable texture.
- **Storage**: up to 1 week in fridge.

6) CRÈME FRAÎCHE – METHOD: NATURAL FERMENTATION

Ingredients(1qt / ≈1L)

- Fresh cream (non-UHT): 1 pt (500 mL)
- Plain yogurt or buttermilk: 2 tbsp (30 g)

Step-by-Step

Warm cream to 95 °F (35 °C).

Add yogurt/buttermilk; stir.

Cover; ferment 12–24 h @ 68–72 °F (20–22 °C).

Stir and refrigerate; thickens further.

Recommended Method

- **Standard**: 18 h → mildly tangy, velvety.
- **Use**: perfect for soups, sauces, desserts.

8.2.2 PLANT-BASED (6 RECIPES)

1) COCONUT YOGURT — METHOD: INCUBATION

Ingredients (1 qt / ≈1L;yields~28–30fl oz / 850–900 mL)

- Full-fat coconut milk (canned, no additives): 1 qt (≈1 L)
- Agar agar powder: 1 tsp (3 g)
- Starter (probiotic capsule or 3 tbsp soy yogurt): 30–45 g

Step-by-Step

- Heat coconut milk to 185 °F (85 °C); whisk in agar.
- Cool to 108–110 °F (42–43 °C).
- Inoculate with probiotics or soy yogurt. Incubate 8–12 h at 104–110 °F (40–43 °C).
- Refrigerate; thickens further.

Recommended Method

- **Standard**:10h →creamy texture.
- **Note**: shake/stir before serving, tends to separate.

2) SOY YOGURT — METHOD: INCUBATION

Ingredients(1qt / ≈1L)

- Unsweetenedsoy milk:1 qt (≈1 L)
- Starter (2–3 tbsp soy yogurt or probiotic capsule):30–45 g

Step-by-Step

- Heat soymilk to 185 °F (85 °C); cool to 108 °F (42 °C).
- Add starter; stir.
- Incubate 6–10 h at 104–110 °F (40–43 °C). Chill 12 h in fridge.

Recommended Method

- **Standard**: 8 h →balanced tang.
- **Storage**: 5–7 days.

3) ALMOND YOGURT — METHOD: INCUBATION

Ingredients(1qt / ≈1L)

- Unsweetened almondmilk (homemade preferred): 1 qt (≈1 L) Agar agar: ½ tsp (2 g)
- Probiotics or plant yogurt: 2–3 tbsp (30–45 g)

Step-by-Step

- Heatalmond milk to 185 °F (85 °C); dissolve agar.
- Cool to 108 °F (42 °C).
- Add starter; stir.
  Incubate 8–12 h.
  Refrigerate.

Recommended Method

- **Standard**:8–10h → light texture.
- **Note**: almond milk is low-protein → thinner yogurt.

4)CASHEW CREAM CHEESE – METHOD: NATURAL FERMENTATION

Ingredients (yields ~14 oz / 400 g)

- Rawcashews: 1.1 lb (500g),soaked 6–8 h
- Filtered water: ½–1 cup (120–240 mL)
- Probiotic powder: 1 capsule or 1 tsp
- Salt: ½ tsp (3 g)

Step-by-Step

- Blend soaked cashews + water into smooth cream.
- Add probiotics + salt.
- Cover with cloth; ferment 24–36 h at room temp.
- Refrigerate; thickensfurther.

Recommended Method

- **Standard**: 24 h →mild tang.
- **Longer**:36 h → sharper flavor, firmer.

5) SUNFLOWER-SEED SPREAD – METHOD: NATURAL FERMENTATION

Ingredients (yields ~14 oz / 400 g)

- Hulled sunflowerseeds:1.1lb(500g), soaked 4–6 h
- Filtered water: ½–1 cup (120–240 mL)
- Probiotic powder: 1 capsule
- Salt: ½ tsp (3 g)

Step-by-Step

- Blend soaked seeds + water.
- Mix in probiotics + salt.
- Cover; ferment 24 h.
- Refrigerate; use as spread.

Recommended Method

- **Standard** :24 h → nutty flavor.
- **Storage** :up to 1 week in fridge.

6)OAT YOGURT – METHOD: INCUBATION

Ingredients (1 qt / ≈1 L)

- Unsweetened oat milk:1 qt (≈1 L)
- Agar agar: 1 tsp (3 g)
- Starter (probiotic or soy yogurt): 2–3 tbsp (30–45 g)

Step-by-Step

- Heat oat milk to 185 °F (85 °C); add agar.
- Cool to 108 °F (42 °C).
- Add starter; stir.
- Incubate 8–12 h.
- Refrigerate.

Recommended Method

- **Standard** :10 h → mild tang, soft texture.
- **Note** :delicate flavor, pairs well with fresh fruit.

CHAPTER 9

NON-ALCOHOLIC PROBIOTIC DRINKS (12 RECIPES)

9.1 METHODS & STEP-BY-STEP PROCEDURES

9.1.1 WATER KEFIR (F1/F2), GINGER BUG, BOTTLE SAFETY

Water Kefir

- Starter: water kefir grains, a living symbiotic mix of bacteria and yeasts.
- First Fermentation (F1): base ferment in sugar water.
  - Ratio: 3–4 tbsp (45–60 g) grains per 1 qt (≈1 L) water.
  - Sugar: 3–4 tbsp (45–60 g); add dried figs or raisins as nutrients.
  - Time: 24–48 h at 68–75 °F (20–24 °C).

Second Fermentation (F2): bottled ferment with flavorings/fruit.

- Strain out grains after F1.
- Transfer liquid to swing-top bottle with fruit, ginger, spices, or juice.
- Ferment 24–48 h at room temp.

Ginger Bug

- Starter:wild culture from fresh ginger + sugar.

  Procedure:

  - Grate 1 tbsp (≈15 g) fresh ginger (with peel).
  - Mix with 1 tbsp (≈15 g) sugar + 2–3 tbsp water.
  - Cover with cloth; feed daily with 15 g ginger + 15 g sugar.
  - After 4–6 days, bubbles and tangy aroma appear → ready to inoculate lemonade, juices, or tea.

Bottle Safety

- Bottle fermentation builds CO_2 pressure → explosion risk.

  Practical rules:

  - Use thick glass (beer/kombucha bottles), never thin glass.
  - Fill only ¾ full, leaving 1–2 in (2–5 cm) headspace.
  - "Burp" bottles (slightly open) every 24 h if unrefrigerated.
  - Refrigerate as soon as desired fizz is reached.
  - If unsure: use food-grade plastic bottles to test pressure (they harden when ready).

9.2.1 WATER KEFIR (5 RECIPES)

1) BASE — METHOD: F1 + F2

Ingredients (1 qt / ≈1L;yields~28–30fl oz / 850–900 mL)

- Filtered water: 1 qt (≈1 L)
- Sugar: 3 tbsp (≈45 g)
- Water kefir grains: 3–4 tbsp (45–60 g) (Optional) 1 dried fig or 2–3 raisins

Step-by-Step

- Dissolve sugar in water; add grains + dried fruit.
- Cover with cloth; ferment 24–48 h @ 68–75 °F (20–24 °C).
- Strain grains → F1 ready to drink or move to F2.
- For F2: transfer liquid to swing-top bottle; ferment 24 h at room temp.

Recommended Method

- **Standard**: 24 h F1 + 24 h F2 → light fizz.
- **Longer**: 48 h F1 → sharper, less sweet.

2) LEMON-GINGER KEFIR — METHOD: FLAVORED F2

Ingredients(1qt / ≈1L)

- Base kefir F1: 1 qt (≈1 L)
- Fresh lemon juice: 3 tbsp (45 mL)
- Fresh ginger slices: 0.35 oz (10 g)
- (Optional) Honey: 1 tsp (5 g)

Step-by-Step

- Prepare base F1 kefir; strain grains.
- Transfer liquid to bottle; add lemon + ginger.
- Ferment 24 h at room temp (F2).
- Refrigerate; serve chilled.

Recommended Method

- **Standard**: 24 h F2 → bright, refreshing.
- **Note**: burp bottle daily for safety.

3) BERRY FIZZ KEFIR — METHOD: FLAVORED F2

Ingredients(1qt / ≈1L)

- Base kefir F1: 1 qt (≈1 L)
- Mixed berries (blueberries, blackberries, raspberries): ½ cup (≈75 g)
- (Optional) Sugar: 1 tsp (5 g) for extra fizz

Step-by-Step

- Transfer base F1 kefir to bottle.
- Add berries.
- Ferment 24–36 h at room temp.
- Strain fruit; refrigerate.

Recommended Method

- **Standard**: 24 h → bright color, fruity.
- **Longer**: 36 h → drier, less sweet.

4) PINEAPPLE-MINT KEFIR — METHOD: FLAVORED F2

Ingredients(1qt / ≈1L)

- Base kefir F1: 1 qt (≈1 L)
- Fresh pineapple cubes: ½ cup (≈80 g)
- Fresh mint leaves: 4–5 leaves

Step-by-Step

- Transfer base F1 kefir to bottle.
- Add pineapple + mint.
- Ferment 24 h at room temp.
- Strain; refrigerate.

Recommended Method

- **Standard**: 24 h → tropical, refreshing.
- **Note**: best consumed within 3–4 days.

5)APPLE-CINNAMON KEFIR —METHOD: FLAVORED F2

Ingredients (1 qt / ≈1 L)

- Base kefir F1: 1 qt (≈1 L)
- Green apple, thinly sliced: ½ cup (≈75 g)
- Small cinnamon stick: 1 (≈2–3 g)

Step-by-Step

- Transfer base F1 kefir to bottle.
- Add apple + cinnamon.
- Ferment 24 h at room temp.
- Strain; refrigerate.

Recommended Method

- **Standard**: 24 h → spiced and crisp.
- **Note**: avoid fermenting >24 h with cinnamon (can turn bitter).

9.2.2 GINGER BUG & SODAS (4 RECIPES)

1) GINGER ALE — METHOD: GINGER BUG + F2

Ingredients (1 qt / ≈1L;yields~28–30fl oz / 850–900 mL)

- Active ginger bug: ¼ cup (≈60 mL, liquid + culture)
- Fresh grated ginger: 2 tbsp (≈30 g)
- Sugar: 3 tbsp (≈45 g)
- Filtered water: 1 qt (≈1 L)

Step-by-Step

- Boil half the water with sugar + ginger; cool.
- Combine with remaining water + ginger bug.
- Transfer to swing-top bottle.
- Ferment 24–48 h at room temp.
- Chill when fizzy.

Recommended Method

- **Standard**: 24 h → sweet, lightly fizzy.
- **Longer**: 36–48 h → drier, tangier.

2)SPARKLINGLEMON — METHOD: GINGER BUG + F2

Ingredients (1 qt / ≈1 L)

- Active ginger bug: ¼ cup (≈60 mL)
- Fresh lemon juice: ¼ cup (≈60 mL)
- Sugar: 3 tbsp (≈45 g)
- Filtered water: to 1 qt (≈1 L)

Step-by-Step

- Dissolve sugar in small amount of hot water; cool.
- Mix with lemon juice + ginger bug.
- Bottle tightly.
- Ferment 24 h at room temp.
- Chill before serving.

Recommended Method

- **Standard**: 24 h → crisp, refreshing soda.
- **Note**: burp bottle daily for safety.

3)SPICED APPLE SODA — METHOD: GINGER BUG + F2

Ingredients (1 qt / ≈1 L)

- Active ginger bug: ¼ cup (≈60 mL)
- Fresh apple juice: 2 cups (≈500 mL)
- Filtered water: 2 cups (≈500 mL)
- Small cinnamon stick: 1 (≈2–3 g)
- (Optional) Whole cloves: 2–3

Step-by-Step

- Mix apple juice + water.
- Add ginger bug + spices.
- Bottle tightly.
- Ferment 24–36 h at room temp.
- Strain spices; refrigerate.

Recommended Method

- **Standard**: 24 h → sweet, spiced.
- **Longer**: 36 h → fizzier, less sweet.

4)BLUEBERRY-LIME SODA — METHOD: GINGER BUG + F2

Ingredients(1qt / ≈1L)

- Active ginger bug: ¼ cup (≈60 mL)
- Fresh blueberries (lightly crushed): ½ cup (≈75 g)
- Fresh lime juice: 2 tbsp (≈30 mL)
- Sugar: 2 tbsp (≈30 g)
- Filtered water: to 1 qt (≈1 L)

Step-by-Step

- Dissolve sugar in small amount of hot water; cool.
- Combine with lime juice, blueberries, and ginger bug.
- Bottle tightly.
- Ferment 24–36 h at room temp.
- Strain berries; refrigerate.

Recommended Method

- Standard: 24 h → fruity, refreshing.
- **Longer**: 36 h → drier, stronger fizz.

9.2.3 KVASS (3 RECIPES)

1)CLASSIC BEET KVASS — METHOD: BRINE FERMENTATION

Ingredients (1 qt / ≈1 L; yields ~28–30 fl oz / 850–900 mL)

- Raw red beets, peeled, diced 1 in (2–3 cm): 1 lb (450 g)
- Sea salt: 0.9 oz (25 g) → 2.5% in 34 fl oz / 1,000 mL water
- Filtered water: enough to cover (~1 qt / 1 L) (Optional) Garlic clove: 1, lightly crushed

Step-by-Step

- Dice beets evenly.
- Place in jar with garlic if using.
- Add 2.5% brine; leave ¾–1 in (2–3 cm) headspace.
- Ferment 3–5 days @ 64–72 °F (18–22 °C).
- Strain; refrigerate.

Recommended Method

- **Standard**:3–4days →earthy, lightly salty.
- **Longer**: 5–7 days → sharper tang.

2) GOLDEN BEET & TURMERIC KVASS — METHOD: SPICED BRINE

Ingredients(1qt / ≈1L)

- Raw golden beets, diced 1 in (2–3 cm): 1 lb (450 g)
- Fresh turmeric root, sliced: 0.35 oz (10 g)
  Sea salt: 0.9 oz (25 g) → 2.5% in 1 L water
- Filtered water: enough to cover
- (Optional) Black peppercorns: 3–4

Step-by-Step

- Dice beets; add turmeric (and pepper if used).
- Cover with 2.5% brine; leave headspace.
- Ferment 3–4 days @ 68–72 °F (20–22 °C).
- Strain; refrigerate.

Recommended Method

- **Standard**: 3 days → golden color, spiced flavor.
- **Longer**: 5 days → tangier, stronger spice.

3) CARROT-APPLE KVASS – METHOD: BRINE FERMENTATION

Ingredients(1qt / ≈1L)

- Fresh carrots, sliced ½ in (1–1.5 cm): 0.66 lb (300 g)
- Crisp apples, thin slices: 0.66 lb (300 g)
- Sea salt: 0.9 oz (25 g) → 2.5% in 1 L water
- Filtered water: enough to cover
- (Optional) Small cinnamon stick: 1

Step-by-Step

- Prep carrots + apples; place in jar.
- Add cinnamon if desired.
- Cover with 2.5% brine.
- Ferment 2–4 days @ 64–72 °F (18–22 °C).
- Strain; refrigerate.

Recommended Method

- **Standard**: 2–3 days → fresh, fruity.
- **Longer**: 4 days → drier, tangier.

Kvass General Notes

- **Normal**: fine bubbles, vivid color, earthy-fresh aroma.
- **Not normal:** fuzzy/colored mold, rotten/solvent smell → discard.
- **Use**: digestive tonic, base for cold soups (e.g., borscht), or refreshing drink.

CHAPTER 10

SOURDOUGH & FERMENTED BATTERS (8 RECIPES)

10.1 METHODS & STEP-BY-STEP PROCEDURES

10.1.1 STARTING A CULTURE, FEEDINGS, HYDRATION MANAGEMENT, LONG PROOFS

Starting a culture (sourdough starter)

- **Basic ingredients**:whole-grainflour (rye or wheat) + filtered water.
- **Standard procedure (Day 1–5):**
  - **Day 1**:mix100gwholeflour+ 100 g water in a glass jar. Cover with breathable cloth.
  - **Days 2–5:** discard half daily and feed with 100 g flour + 100 g water.
  - **By Day 5–7:** bubbles, tangy aroma, and volume increase → ready to bake.

Feedings

- **Frequency**:every24 h at room temp (68–75 °F / 20–24 °C) or every 5–7 days in fridge.
- **Standard ratio:** 1part starter : 1 part flour : 1 part water (e.g., 100 g each).
- **Note:** consistentfeedings maintain balance of lactobacilli + yeasts.

Hydration management

- **Hydration** =water/flour ratio.
- **100% hydration:** 1:1 water to flour → soft, versatile starter.
- **65–75% hydration:** stiffer starter, good for rustic breads.
- **125% hydration**:liquid starter, best for fermented batters (e.g., dosa, pancakes).

Long proofs

- Naturally leavened breads benefit from extended fermentation (12–24 h).
- Bulk fermentation (first rise): 4–6 h at room temp or 12–18 h in fridge.
- Final proof (second rise): 2–4 h at room temp or 8–12 h in fridge.
- Note: long proofs improve structure, aroma complexity, and digestibility.

Safety & Practical Notes

- **Healthy starter**:finebubbles, yogurt/green-apple aroma.
- **Discard if:** solvent/rottensmell, colored mold.
- **Always use clean utensils;** avoid contamination.

10.2.1 STARTERS (2 RECIPES)

1) WHEATSTARTER—METHOD: 100%HYDRATION

Ingredients (yields ≈1 qt / 1 L mature starter)

- Whole or semi-whole wheat flour: 100 g daily
- Filtered water: 100 g daily (≈100 mL)

Step-by-Step

- **Day 1:** mix 100 g flour + 100 g water in 1 qt (1 L) glass jar. Cover with breathable cloth. **Day 2:** discard half; feed with 100 g flour + 100 g water.
- **Days 3–5:** repeat every 24 h.
- **From Day 4 onward:** culture should double in 6–8 h after feeding, with fine bubbles and tangy aroma.

Recommended Method

- **Standard**: keep at 68–75 °F (20–24 °C) for balanced development.
- **Stronger**: whole wheat flour → more vigorous activity.
- **Storage**: once mature, refrigerate and feed every 5–7 days.

2)RYESTARTER — METHOD: 100% HYDRATION

Ingredients (yields ≈1 qt / 1 L mature starter)

- **Whole rye flour:** 100 g daily
- **Filtered water:** 100 g daily (≈100 mL)

Step-by-Step

- **Day 1:** mix 100 g rye flour + 100 g water in 1 qt (1 L) jar. Cover with cloth.
- **Day 2:** discard half; feed with 100 g flour + 100 g water.
- **Days 3–5:** repeat daily.
- **From Day 3:** rye ferments faster → culture may already be active by Day 3–4.

Recommended Method

- **Standard**: 3–5 days @ 68–75 °F (20–24 °C).
- **Note**: rye has more active amylase enzymes → vigorous fermentation, ideal for rustic/dense breads.
- **Storage**: refrigerate with weekly feedings; bring to room temp and feed 1–2 times before baking.

10.2.2 BREAD & FOCACCIA (3 RECIPES)

1) EVERYDAY SOURDOUGH — METHOD: DIRECT MIX

Ingredients (1 loaf ~1.5 lb / 700 g)

- Bread flour (or Type 0 wheat flour): 500 g
- Wheat starter (100% hydration): 100 g
- Filtered water: 325 g (65% hydration)
- Fine sea salt: 10 g

Step-by-Step

- Mix flour + water; autolyse 30 min.
- Add starter + salt; knead until smooth.
- Bulk ferment: 4–5 h @ 75 °F (24 °C) with 2–3 folds.
- Shape loaf; proof 2 h.
- Bake in preheated oven 475 °F (245 °C), in Dutch oven: 20 min covered + 20 min uncovered.

Recommended Method

- **Standard**: 65% hydration, easy to handle.
- **Higher hydration(70%):** more open crumb, thinner crust.

2) COUNTRY LOAF — METHOD: LONG FERMENTATION

Ingredients (1 large loaf ~2 lb / 900 g)

- Bread flour (Type 0): 700 g Whole
- Grain flour (wheat/rye): 100 g Rye
- Starter (100% hydration): 150 g
- Filtered water: 560 g (70% hydration)
- Salt: 15 g

Step-by-Step

- Autolyse: flour + water; rest 45 min.
- Add starter + salt; knead.
- Bulk ferment: 5–6 h @ 72 °F (22 °C) with folds every 30–45 min.
- Pre-shape + rest 30 min.
- Shape; place in floured banneton.
- Final proof: 12–14 h in fridge.
- Bake 20 min covered + 25 min uncovered @ 475 °F (245 °C).

Recommended Method

- **Standard**: 12 h fridge → balanced tang, open structure.
- **Longer**: up to 18 h → stronger acidity, deeper flavor.

3) LONG-RISE FOCACCIA — METHOD: HIGH HYDRATION

Ingredients(9×13in / 23×33cmpan)

- Bread flour (Type 0): 500 g
- Wheat starter (100% hydration): 100 g
- Filtered water: 400 g (80% hydration)
- Salt: 12 g
- Extra virgin olive oil: 40 g (+ more for topping)
- Fresh rosemary + coarse salt: to taste

Step-by-Step

- Mix flour + water + starter; rest 30 min.
- Add salt + oil; knead briefly.
- Bulk ferment: 4 h @ 75 °F (24 °C) with folds in bowl.
- Transfer to oiled pan; stretch gently.
- Final proof: 12–16 h in fridge, covered.
- Before baking: dimple surface, top with oil, rosemary, salt.
- Bake at 450 °F (230 °C) for 25–30 min until golden.

Recommended Method

- **Standard**: 12 h fridge → airy crumb, crisp edges.
- **Longer**: 16 h → deeper flavor, light tang.

10.2.3 CRÊPES & PANCAKES (2 RECIPES)

1) SOURDOUGH PANCAKES – METHOD: FERMENTED BATTER

Ingredients (≈10 medium pancakes)

- Active starter (100% hydration): 200 g
- Milk or plant-based milk: 120 g
- Large egg: 1
- Sugar: 1 tbsp (15 g)
- Melted butter or neutral oil: 1 tbsp (15 g)
- Flour: 100 g
- Salt: ¼ tsp (1 g)
- (Optional) Baking soda: ½ tsp for extra fluffiness

Step-by-Step

- In bowl, mix starter + milk + egg + sugar + butter.
- Add flour + salt; whisk into smooth batter.
- Rest 30–60 min at room temp.
- Cook on lightly greased skillet, 2–3 min per side.

Recommended Method

- **Standard**:useafter30–60 min → mild flavor.
- **Longer ferment:** cover and refrigerate 8–12 h → tangier, fluffier pancakes.

2) SOURDOUGH CRÊPES —METHOD: THIN FERMENTED BATTER

Ingredients (≈10 thin crêpes)

- Active starter (100% hydration): 150 g
- Milk or plant-based milk: 250 g
- Large eggs: 2
- Flour: 100 g
- Salt: ¼ tsp (1 g)
- Melted butter (or neutral oil): 1 tbsp (15 g)

Step-by-Step

- Mix starter + milk + eggs.
- Add flour + salt + butter; whisk until smooth, thin batter.
- Rest 30 min at room temp.
- Heat non-stick pan; lightly grease.
- Pour ¼ cup batter, swirl pan for thin layer.
- Cook 1–2 min per side.

Recommended Method

- **Standard**: 30 min rest → delicate, neutral crêpes.
- **Long rest:** 8 h in fridge → tangier, richer flavor.

10.2.4 FLATBREAD (1 RECIPE)

SOURDOUGH FLATBREAD (PIADINA-STYLE) — METHOD: DIRECT MIX

Ingredients (8 medium flatbreads)

- Bread flour (or Type 0 wheat flour): 400 g
- Wheat starter (100% hydration): 100 g
- Warm water: 150 g
- Extra virgin olive oil (or lard for traditional style): 40 g
- Fine sea salt: 8 g

Step-by-Step

- Mix flour + water + starter into rough dough.
- Add oil + salt; knead until smooth.
- Ferment 2–3 h at room temp (75 °F / 24 °C) → partial rise.
- Divide into 8 balls; rest 30 min covered.
- Roll each ball into thin disk (≈20 cm).
- Cook on hot griddle/skillet without fat: 1–2 min per side.

Recommended Method

- **Standard**: 2–3 h → soft, mildly tangy flatbreads.
- **Cold proof:** refrigerate dough 8–12 h → deeper flavor, easier digestibility.
- **Use**: fill with cheese, vegetables, cured meats, or hummus/salads for plant-based version.

CONCLUSION

This book has taken us on a journey from the simplest beginnings — brines, fruit and vegetable ferments — all the way to more complex preparations such as long-fermented breads, probiotic drinks, and plant-based dairy alternatives. Each chapter has provided clear tools, precise ratios, and, most importantly, the freedom to adapt processes to personal taste, seasonality, and available ingredients. What unites all these recipes is the principle of natural fermentation: an ancient, accessible, and sustainable process that transforms everyday ingredients into living foods, rich in nutrients and unique in flavor. It is not just about following instructions, but about learning to tune into the timing, aromas, textures, and variations that nature offers. The recipes here are not rigid formulas but rather starting points. Each cook is encouraged to adapt, experiment with new combinations, and find their own balance between acidity, sweetness, and freshness. Home fermentation is as much an art as it is a science: it requires precision in ratios but leaves room for creativity and intuition. The true result is not only a collection of dishes but also a shift in how we approach food: with more care, awareness, and respect for natural processes. Bringing ferments to the table means enriching not only our meals but also our everyday well-being.

BONUSES

Unlock Your Exclusive Bonus Pack!

As a valued reader of this cookbook, you now have access to a collection of FREE companion resources designed to make fermentation easier, safer, and more creative:

- Say goodbye to dead cultures with the **Starter Care & Rescue Kit**
- Stay in control with **Photocopiable Batch Sheets** (Small-Batch / Family)
- Unlock chef-level flavor with the **Flavor Pairing & Brine Spice Atlas**
- Turn garden bounty into perfect jars with the **Garden-to-Jar Planner & Yield/Cost Calculator**

- Taste Asia at home with **Authentic Ferments Collection**
- Boost your health with the **Superfood Ferment Pack**:
- 15 Powerhouse RecipesFix any ferment fast with **Visual Troubleshooting Guide**

How to get your bonuses:

Please email **summitpressbooks@gmail.com** with the BOOK TITLE in the subject line, and include your request in the message.

Don't miss out!

You already have the cookbook — now claim the extra tools that make it complete. Because your pantry deserves the very best, every single day.

YOUR OPINION MATTERS

THANK YOU FOR YOUR PURCHASE!!

A Quick Favor Before You Go

Every review helps other home cooks and wellness-minded readers make a more informed choice when looking for a clear, trustworthy guide to fermentation.

A few honest lines on Amazon are enough to share your experience with this book: which recipes you enjoyed, which instructions felt especially clear, or how the step-by-step guidance helped you feel more confident in your kitchen.

An honest review does not need to be long or perfect. It only needs to reflect your real experience.

Thank you for choosing this cookbook and for bringing the world of fermented foods into your home.

Your feedback is truly appreciated and may help someone else begin their own journey toward more flavorful, nourishing, homemade food.

SCAN TO REVIEW

Takes 5 seconds!

Access it now before you forget!

NEED HELP?
Feel free to email me:
summitpressbooks@gmail.com

BUILT BY:
ELYRA J. CAVENDENE

We're here to help you succeed.

Made in the USA
Las Vegas, NV
03 November 2026

57405435R00066